# Contents

PRELUDE: **Practice Swings**...........5

FIRST HOLE: **In the Beginning**...........9

SECOND HOLE: **The Ball and the Word**...........23

THIRD HOLE: **Church Pews and Trinities**...........29

FOURTH HOLE: **Grand Slams and Gospels**...........39

FIFTH HOLE: **Payne Stewart and Palm Sunday**...........49

SIXTH HOLE: **Golf and Bethlehem**...........57

SEVENTH HOLE: **The Number of Plenty**...........65

EIGHTH HOLE: **Claret Jug, Cup of Wine**...........71

NINTH HOLE: **Learn at the Turn**...........79

TENTH HOLE: **The Pulpit**...........87

ELEVENTH HOLE: **Saint Andrew—Course and Man**...........99

TWELFTH HOLE: **Augusta and Apostles**...........109

THIRTEENTH HOLE: **The Amen Corner**...........119

FOURTEENTH HOLE: **Clubs and Talents**...........125

FIFTEENTH HOLE: **The Sistine Chapel of Golf**...........133

SIXTEENTH HOLE: **Miracles of Golf and God**...........145

SEVENTEENTH HOLE: **Golf's Greatest**...........159

EIGHTEENTH HOLE: **Valley of Sin, Death on a Cross**...........175

NINETEENTH HOLE: **The Clubhouse**...........187

POSTLUDE: **Another Round?**...........191

SOURCES AND PERMISSIONS...........193

INDICES...........201

# Practice Swings

As most anyone who plays the game will tell you: Golf is a religious experience. After all, other than at a place of worship, you won't find God's name evoked more often or with such passion than on the links. Of course, on the course most references to the Almighty are in reaction to shots landing in woods, hazards or traps rather than fairways, greens or holes. Still, there is a great deal the Word of God can teach us about this game of golf, and vice versa.

If, like the apostle Thomas, you find yourself doubting, then consider the number four. This digit plays a big part in the Good Book and the great game. Off the tee there are four major tournaments that make up the sport's Grand Slam—the Masters, U.S. Open, British Open and PGA Championship. Matching the game's holy quartet are the four gospels of the New Testament detailing the life, death and resurrection of Jesus Christ. To most any golf fan the singular names of Ben, Arnie, Jack and Tiger call to mind long drives, miraculous shots and thrilling finishes to major championships. Similarly, for the faithful the names of Matthew, Mark, Luke and John elicit memories of miracles, words to live by, and the most incredible finish of all, the triumph over death by the son of God.

At this point, I should point out that I am not a biblical scholar or a theological expert by any means. I am even less of a golfer. In my first ever round of golf I posted a 74. Most weekend golfers would be envious of that total—until they learned that it defined my handicap. My total stroke count actually equaled 144. To the numerically minded, 144 represents a gross. Even though I was a high school student at the time, that term also described my play. Put another way, it took me more than twice as many shots per hole as what was par for the course. I'd like to say that the precarious pin positions of Pebble Beach had a great deal to do with my over-inflated tally. I'd like to say that, but then I'd be lying. No, my efforts were confounded by a par 70 municipal course with nary a Postage Stamp, Punch Bowl or Island Green within its borders.

My scores have come down (somewhat) since then, though the game still provides more challenges per hole than I'd care to admit. With regularity I land in more rough than fairways, clear more fences than water hazards, and hit more trees than greens. Quite frankly, many years ago, at the opening hole of a nine-hole course in North Seattle, a towering drive of mine landed on the roof of a nearby gas station. Just call me Captain Hook. With my second shot, however, I found my ball actually on the green, a mere two feet from the cup.

A towering drive of mine landed on the roof of a nearby gas station.

Since this book in part is about the Bible, honesty compels me to point out that the cup in question was on the second hole and I was still playing the first.

Despite these shot shortcomings, I find myself enamored of the beauty of the world's most wondrous courses and stand in awe of the professionals who play them. Upon delving into the history and traditions of the game, I find that there is a great deal that can be learned about a hole in one and the One True God. Though not a biblical scholar or scratch golfer, I consider myself a student of scripture and sport, hoping to learn more about each with every passing day. I hope that this book encourages you to do the same.

At the 2007 PGA Championship, held at Southern Hills Country Club in Tulsa, Oklahoma, story lines spoke equally of heat, hazards and heartache. Temperatures reached triple digits (perhaps reflecting my own golf scores), calling to mind the 1958 U.S. Open played on this same course in much the same conditions. At that time, Tommy Bolt kept his cool, winning what has come to be called the Blast Furnace Open. Twelve years later, when Dave Stockton won the 1970 PGA, Tulsa temperatures reached 112 degrees. Should players survive the heat, there is still the rather imposing sand bunker, dogleg and blind water hazard of Southern Hills' notable 12th hole with which to contend. This PGA represented the last chance for Tiger Woods, the sport's dominant player, to win a major that year. Atop the leader board after the first day's play were Graeme Storm, who had once worked at a cake factory after losing his European playing card, and John Daly, who spent the day before preparing for the tournament by visiting a local casino. (Perhaps there's hope for us all!)

Even more surprising than the early leaders was the fact that the world's best golfer, Tiger Woods, found himself six strokes back with a one under par 71, hardly an enviable position for anyone trying to win the prestigious PGA. But golf, like life, is not judged by one shot or one day's score, but by progress made during the course of one's sporting or spiritual journey.

In Tiger's case, he came roaring back on day two with a mind-boggling 63—a score that tied the record for lowest tally during a major championship—giving him a lead he would never relinquish, not to mention his fourth PGA Championship. Thus, not only did the tournament offer heroic shot making but a biblical lesson as well. Messrs. Woods and Daly just happen to exemplify the parable of the talents, where one man nurtures his talent and is rewarded while another wastes (buries) what has been given to him and loses all. Leave it to the Almighty to place valuable life lessons inside a golf bag next to the dimpled white balls and painted wooden tees.

That's what this book is all about—the many remarkable, mystical connections that sport and Spirit, links and Lord, game and God share. For instance, both have a Saint Andrew, church pews, and descriptions of hell, whether deep bunkers or everlasting fire. Golf speaks of the Amen Corner and the Valley of Sin. The Bible refers to Bethpage and woods, or at least branches. There's a lot to be learned on the greens and in the scriptures about Claret Jugs and cups of wine, sixth holes and the sixth Psalm, hazards of play and the forgiveness of sins.

So what are you waiting for? God says: Tee it up! The following "18 Holes" are like the best courses in the world: fun, challenging, and worth playing again and again.

# In the Beginning

Step into the batter's box of any major league baseball stadium, whether venerable Fenway Park in Boston or historic Wrigley Field in Chicago, and the pitcher stands 60 feet, 6 inches away. Break a huddle on the frozen tundra of Lambeau Field in Green Bay or the sun-drenched grass of Dolphin Stadium in Miami, and there are still ten yards to go for a first down. Take a bounce pass on a fast break in the seventh game of the NBA finals at Madison Square Garden in New York or Staples Center in Los Angeles, and whether by finger roll, lay up off the glass or dunk you very much, the ball still must go through a rim 10 feet above the court.

Now step to the first tee of a golf course and you could be facing a 346-yard, par 4 across the gorse and heather of the links at Prestwick near Edinburgh. Or maybe a 404-yard, par 4 from an elevated tee at Cherry Hills outside of Denver. Or perhaps a 600-yard, par 5 dogleg at Spyglass Hill at Pebble Beach. In short, medium and long, these are three different courses with three distinct opening holes.

That there are as many different first holes as there are golf courses—a recent count put that number at 32,000 worldwide[1]—is worthy of wonder. That each course has 18 holes to be played, each as singular as the three described above, adds further evidence to the claim that golf is, indeed, a unique game every time you play it.

What makes the sport even more extraordinary is that it can teach us a great deal about spirituality. Skeptical? Consider such evocative phrases that describe aspects of some of the game's most famous holes: Valley of Sin, Church Pews, The Pulpit, Hell's Half

Acre and the Amen Corner. The sport and the Scriptures each have their own Lord—Byron and Jesus respectively. For every miraculous shot on the golf course, there is a true miracle performed by the Son of God. Jesus even taught his disciples the spiritual version of a mulligan: Instead of one free do over on the golf course, Peter had *three* chances to acknowledge Jesus the night before he died, and *three more* to answer Jesus' question after the Resurrection, *"Do you love me?"* (see John 18:15-27; 21:15-19).

With centuries of players and matches in golf books and millennia of prayers and teachings in the Good Book, one may ponder where to first search for connections between the holes and the holy. To fully appreciate the many and varied connections between golf and God, it helps to take a clue from scripture itself, specifically the first three words of the Book of Genesis, the opening book of the Holy Bible: *In the beginning* (Genesis 1:1).

For every miraculous shot on the golf course, there is a true miracle performed by the Son of God.

Long before the turn of the century and the Model T, golf was. Before the Civil War, golf was. Heck, before the American Revolutionary War, golf was. As a matter of fact, before Columbus sailed the ocean blue and discovered America, you guessed it, golf was. The first game of golf for which there are records dates back to 1456 at the Bruntsfield Links in Edinburgh, Scotland.[2] Again, that's a course for which there are records. Historians have found traces of the game having been played in China as early as the 11th century and in the Netherlands two hundred years later.[3] However, golf historians and traditionalists consider Scotland of the 1100s as the birthplace of the game.

If the fact that golf is 900 years old is surprising, get ready for something truly unfathomable. For the origin of the Almighty, the Old Testament provides a firsthand account. When Moses encountered God as the burning bush, as told in the Book of Exodus, he asked a logical question, only to receive an answer that still defies all logic: *But Moses said to God, "If I come to the Israelites and say to them, 'The God of your ancestors has sent me to you,' and they ask me, 'What is his name?' what shall I say to them?" God said to Moses, "I AM WHO I AM." He said further, "Thus, you shall say to the Israelites, 'I AM has sent me to you'"* (Exodus 3:13-14).

God's own name provides the answer, as incomprehensible as it may seem, to a number of questions. Who are you? How long have you been around? Where did you come from? I AM who always has been and always will be. I AM who always is. I AM who had no beginning and has no end.

A parallel introduction takes place in the New Testament. The evangelist John intentionally opens his Gospel with the very same three words that open Genesis. In John's case, he speaks to the origin of Jesus—the Word of God—as a way to confirm the Son's real yet mysterious relationship with the Father: *In the beginning was the Word, and the Word was with God, and the Word was God. He was in the beginning with God. All things came into being through him, and without him not one thing came into being* (John 1:1-3).

So what were these things that came into being? *And God said,*

*"Let the waters under the sky be gathered together into one place, and let the dry land appear." And it was so. God called the dry land Earth and the waters that were gathered together he called Seas. And God saw that it was good. Then God said, "Let the earth put forth vegetation: plants yielding seed, and fruit trees of every kind on earth...." And it was so. The earth brought forth vegetation; plants yielding seed of every kind, and trees of every kind bearing fruit.... And God saw that it was good. And there was evening and there was morning, the third day* (Genesis 1:9-13).

Conservatively speaking, there are somewhere in the neighborhood of 100,000 different species of trees in the world, and 250,000 known species of plants,[4] giving golf course architects plenty to choose from when planning 18 holes. Trees of every kind include the cypress found at Cypress Point at Pebble Beach, California; the Carolina pines of Augusta in Georgia; the palm trees of Mauna Kea on the Big Island of Hawaii; the oak of Oak Tree in Edmond, Oklahoma; and more. Seeds of the earth hold among their numbers those of Kentucky Blue, Red Top, Fescue, Bent and Bermuda grasses, found on many a fairway and green throughout the world.

A great many of golf's well-known hole designs are inspired by the dry lands of God's handiwork. On the third hole at the National in Southampton, one must play blind and clear a jagged hill—the Alps—to the green below. National's third was inspired by the seventeenth at Prestwick, Scotland, which also took its cue from the much taller, stately originals bordering Italy and Switzerland. A huge outcropping of rocks on the eleventh at The Country Club at Brookline takes its name from the tallest mountains in the world, the Himalayas. Large sandy, desolate bunkers such as the seventeenth at Lower Baltusrol are called the Saharas and take their name from the Creator's giant sand trap in Northern Africa. To mark its beginning, Winged Foot calls its first hole Genesis, named after the first book of the Bible.

Of course, God didn't stop with plants and trees: *And God said, "Let the living waters bring forth swarms of living creatures, and let birds fly above the earth across the dome of the sky." So God created the great sea monsters and every living creature that moves, of every kind, with which the waters swarm, and every winged bird of every kind. And God saw that it was good…. And there was evening and there was morning, the fifth day. And God said, "Let the earth bring forth living creatures of every kind: cattle and creeping things and wild animals of the earth of every kind." And it was so. God made the wild animals of the earth of every kind, and everything that creeps upon the ground of every kind. And God saw that it was good* (Genesis 1:20-25).

If God lives by adages, one of his favorites would have to be that variety is the spice of life. Various estimates put the number of species of birdies in the sky to be near 10,000;[5] the types of fish in the sea at 20,000;[6] the number of species of wild animals to be in the neighborhood of 500,000; and kinds of creeping things, which I interpret to be creepy things (insects), about a million.[7]

Golf aficionados marvel at the prodigious drives off the tee by John Daly, often approaching 400 yards. Or feel intimidated by The Pines course at The International near Boston, measuring more than 8,300 yards. Or have trouble comprehending the career winnings of Tiger Woods, in excess of $120 million. However, for sheer mind-boggling numbers, check out God's tally on the fourth day when he created the *"lights in the dome of the sky to give light upon the earth"* (Genesis 1:15). CNN online reported that the Australian National

University put the quantity of stars in the sky at 70 sextillion.[8] That's the number seven followed by 22 zeroes. (At this point, I would like to point out that seven is the biblical number of plenty. And you don't get much more plentiful than 7 with 22 golf balls after it.)

All too often we take for granted that God created the world and everything in it. But when one considers the variety and number of species that have been placed on our planet, a feeling of awe is only natural. Think about the astounding number of stars mentioned above. Just to count to 70 sextillion would take more than two quadrillion years (a two followed by 15 zeroes), considerably less time if one were to count, as Noah of ark fame did, by twos. Is it any wonder we cannot grasp the majesty and power of the Almighty?

Later in Genesis there is mention of the Garden of Eden, an idyllic setting, full of verdant trees, and flowing streams: *And the Lord planted a garden in Eden, in the east.… Out of the ground the Lord God made to grow every tree that is pleasant to the sight.… A river flows out of Eden to water the garden, and from there it divides and becomes four branches* (Genesis 2:8-10).

Close your eyes and you can picture lush lawns, tranquil ponds, rockery, gentle slopes and trees of every kind. Perhaps an Eden of another kind comes to mind, one by the name of Augusta, Greenbrier, even Eden at Saint Andrews. Places where, simply put, all is as it should be.

Each and every Eden of golf has also had its creator—gentlemen of the game who added their architectural expertise to the terrain that Mother Nature and Father God provided. Augusta, Cypress Point and Royal Melbourne owe their beauty to Alister MacKenzie. Albert (A.W.) Tillinghast designed Bethpage Black, Baltusrol Upper and Winged Foot West. Spyglass Hill, Firestone South and Mauna Kea owe their existence to Robert Trent Jones, Sr., while Donald Ross brought Oakmont, Pinehurst #2 and Inverness into being. Arnold Palmer is associated with Bay Hill, Ben Crenshaw with Sand Hills, and Jack Nicklaus with Muirfield Village.

Greens exist amidst the God-given gorse at Saint Andrews. The pounding surf and craggy coast of California define Cypress Point. Sand Hills follows the contours of the Nebraskan plains. Banff Springs Golf Course lies at the base of the beautiful and oh-so-natural Canadian Rockies. Augusta is known for its flowering azaleas; Sawgrass, Bay Hill and Doral are notable for their clear blue waters, inspired by God's own seas.

All of which is to say, from tee box to green, there has been a hand guiding such carefully cultivated, specifically sculpted beauty. Much like the hand of God has guided creation itself.

"In the beginning" can also refer to the opening hole of a golf course. That journey to the primary pin sets the stage for the round that is to follow. From initial tee shot to first putts, a player receives a sense of the conditions of the fairways, the placement of bunkers, traps and water hazards, the length of the rough, and the speed of the greens. While perhaps similar, no two courses are alike in the way they play. Some may open with a rather tame par 3 to ease a player into the round. Others may start with a demanding par 4 to set a challenging tone. Still others may offer a long par 5 to allow golfers to establish a sense of pace. To wit: Thirty minutes west of Glasgow, Scotland, along the Ayrshire coast, is a stretch of land where manicured greens

lie amidst rolling dunes, gorse and heather. Known as Prestwick Golf
Club, the old course is the birthplace of the Open Championship, also
known these days as the British Open, one of the four tournaments
that comprise the Grand Slam of golf. In 1851, a dozen Scotsmen
formed the club and enticed Tom Morris the elder from nearby — and
now legendary — Saint Andrews to become Keeper of the Green, Ball
and Club Maker.[9]

Nine years later, on its 12-hole course, the first Open was played,
won by a gentlemen by the name of Willie Park, who managed a 174
over 36 holes, a score close to my own heart. Old Tom Morris came
in second that year, but won the Open Championship three times in
the next six years. His son, Young Tom Morris, did dad even better,
claiming *his* three titles consecutively from 1868 to 1870. In the last of
these tournaments, Morris tallied a three on the opening gambit en
route to a record 47 over the 12 holes. It should be noted that instead
of an oversized driver with a graphite shaft, Junior played with a
hickory staff and wooden head. Oh, by the way, that first hole was a
par 6, 578-yard affair. That's right. Young Tom carded a double eagle
3 on a 578-yard hole with a wooden stick amidst the spiny gorse of
western Scotland. Take that, Tiger Woods. In claiming three opens in
a row, Morris the younger came to possess the Championship Belt,
made of red Moroccan leather with silver clasps, precursor to the
Claret Jug awarded to the winner of the British Open today.[10]

Prestwick's opening hole more than a century ago is presently
its sixteenth green. Today, the first is aptly called the Railway, for near
the tee is Prestwick Station, with the local railway line running down
the right-hand side of the fairway.[11] Instead of the hush of the gallery
upon teeing off, players often contend with the shrill whistle of a

departing train. Few if any opening holes in all of golf combine such a unique hazard of play with the game's early history.

Traveling west across the pond and beyond to the mile-high environs of the Denver area brings one to the first tee of the Cherry Hills Country Club, site of perhaps the most famous opening shot of a round of golf ever. The year was 1960; the tournament was the U.S. Open. Down seven at the start of the final round, Arnold Palmer decided to try to drive the green of the 404-yard first hole. His monstrous tee shot carried well in the thin air, eluded the creek on the right and bunker on the left, and landed near the pin. Two putts later, Arnie had his first of four straight birdies on way to a 65 and his first and only U.S. Open, one of seven majors he won in his colorful career.[12]

Players often contend with the shrill whistle of a departing train.

For sheer beauty, continue west to the California coast and the 600-yard, par 5-opening hole of Spyglass Hill at Pebble Beach. Length, twin walls of Monterey pines, a sweeping dogleg to the left provide early challenges. Three trees stand guard in the middle of the fairway often stopping balls that have the audacity to approach without proper credentials. Should one negotiate the terrain while still maintaining sanity, the reward is a sweeping view of the Pacific Ocean for as far as the eye can see.

So Prestwick offers rich history, Cherry Hills inspired play, and Spyglass sheer beauty. One expects an interesting opening hole with every golf course. That's part of what makes the game so challenging and unique. But do you know there are different openings to the Bible? It's true. Genesis actually contains two creation stories.

After creating the heavens and the earth on the first day, the sky on the second, the dry land and seas on the third, the sun, moon and the stars on the fourth, the birds of the air and fish of the sea on the fifth, and the wild animals and creeping things on the morning of the sixth, God was ready for his pièce de résistance:

> Then God said, "Let us make humankind in our image, according to our likeness; and let them have dominion over the fish of the sea, over the birds of the air, and over the cattle, and over all the wild animals of the earth, and over every creeping thing that creeps on the earth."
> So God created man in his image;
> in the image of God he created them;
> male and female he created them.
> God blessed them, and God said to them, "Be fruitful and multiply, and fill the earth and subdue it; and have dominion over the fish of the sea, over the birds of he air, and over every living thing that moves on the earth.... And it was so. God saw everything that he had made, and indeed, it was very good. And there was evening and there was morning, the sixth day" (Genesis 1:26-28, 31).

Like a perfectly manicured green, this opening is pretty cut and dried. Or so you would think. In the time it takes a seemingly well-placed putt to lip out of the hole, however, Genesis presents another, alternative version:

> *These are the generations of heavens and the earth when they were created.*
>
> *In the day that the Lord God made the earth and the heavens, when no plant of the field was yet in the earth and no herb of the field had yet sprung up—for the Lord God had not caused it to rain upon the earth; and there was no one to till the ground; but a stream would rise from the earth and water the whole face of the ground—then the Lord God formed man from the dust of the ground, and breathed into his nostrils the breath of life; and the man became a living being* (Genesis 2:4-7).

Subsequently in this version, God created the Garden of Eden and, concluding that man should not be alone, added the animals of the fields and the birds of the air. Then the Almighty caused the man to fall into a deep sleep and performed the first and only "riboscopy" in the history of creation:

> *Then he took one of his ribs, and closed up its place with flesh. And the rib that the Lord God had taken from the man he made into a woman and he brought her to the man.*
>
> *Then the man said:*
> *"This at last is bone of my bones*
> *and flesh of my flesh;*
> *this one shall be called Woman,*
> *for out of Man this one was taken"* (Genesis 2:21-23).

As one can see, there are a few discrepancies in these two accounts. In the first, God created the birds of the sky, the beasts of the earth, and then man and woman together. In the second, he created man first, the creatures second, and woman third. In a way it's like starting one round of golf with a par 4 dogleg to the right and another with a short uphill par 3. Both provide a challenge, both have their rewards. The same can be said about the dual accounts in the Bible.

Genesis presents two creation stories, perhaps for different audiences, perhaps for different times. After all, scripture is not a history book presenting facts but a God-inspired account that constantly reveals itself to its readers throughout the ages. A biblical passage may strike one person a certain way, another person completely differently. A particular scriptural reference may even strike the same person differently depending upon the circumstances surrounding the reader's life when perusing it, just like the same hole in golf may be played differently by one player from round to round depending upon weather and course conditions.

As it is, these two biblical stories offer complementary wisdom regarding our special relationship with God our creator. From the one we learn that God created man and woman together, equal in his eyes. From the other, we see that we are all part of one another on this earth, bound together from the beginning of time.

As Baltusrol has its upper and lower courses, Winged Foot its east and west, and Pinehurst its courses numbered one through eight, so too does the Bible offer creation stories A and B. Each story and course is rich with its own details; all provide learning if we take the time to study the words on the page or the lie of ball. Playing various courses helps improve our game, though we may not realize it at the time. Similarly, the different creation stories can impact our lives in the mysterious way that only the Word of God can do.

In the beginning, too, there's a lot to be learned, whether taking up golf or studying the Bible. Chances are the bunkers and the book will still confound us at times. But if we continue to play and pray, epiphanies await. Greens are easier to read, as are verses. A light goes on regarding our back-swing; the Light of the World illuminates our life.

One last thought. Genesis concludes its first creation story with the now familiar recap of how God took a day off: *Thus the heavens and the earth were finished, and all their multitude. And on the seventh day God finished the work that he had done, and he rested on the seventh day…. So God blessed the seventh day and hallowed it, because on it God rested from all the work that he had done in creation* (Genesis 2:1:3).

Today that seventh day is considered by most Christians to be Sunday, a day of rest and a day to spend time with our Creator in prayer. However, might the Almighty also have created a day of rest so that he and golf fans everywhere could eventually watch the thrilling final rounds of tournaments from around the world?

God only knows.

# The Ball and the Word

Five miles northeast of Hutchinson, Kansas, which is 59 miles northwest of Wichita, is the Perry Maxwell-designed Prairie Dunes Country Club, often called the state's hidden treasure. Maxwell appreciated the "foundations" for his courses that God naturally provided. The architect's approach to design was simple: "A golf course should be there, not brought there."[1] In the case of Prairie Dunes, God bestowed an abundance of riches. After touring the 480-acre site for the course, Maxwell declared, "There are 118 golf holes here and all I have to do is eliminate 100 of them."[2] One of the 18 that survived the cut was the second hole. Maxwell took the landscape of dunes that the Lord laid out and nestled this hole into a small hillside. Natural thickets of undergrowth border the right hand side, and strategically placed bunkers guard the left. Though the hole is a short 161-yard par 3, winds from the plains often augment the challenge that the two-tiered green provides. First opened in 1937, Prairie Dunes preceded the film *The Wizard of Oz* by two years. Had Dorothy been a golfer, chances are she never would have left Kansas in the first place.

In the 1920s, the Shriners of Chicago's Medinah Temple decided to build a golf course worthy of the finest in the land. By the early 1930s, Medinah Country Club had come into being. Hale Irwin won the 1990 U.S. Open at Medinah No. 3, while Tiger Woods captured the PGA Championship there nine years later. Tiger found the course so much to his liking that he repeated his win in 2006. In so doing, Irwin and Woods both navigated the waters of Lake Kadijah, which separate tee from green on the par 3, 192-yard second hole. Kadijah is a form of the Arabic *khadijah*, which means "early baby"[3] or

23

"trustworthy,"[4] though some translate the term to mean "waters that swallow short mid-irons." A bunker at the back of the green further complicates matters.

In 1907, play began on one of the most-respected and appreciated of all golf courses in the world. North Carolina's Pinehurst No. 2 has hosted some of the game's greatest players. In 1940, Ben Hogan defeated Sam Snead in the North and South Open to win his first professional championship. Hogan the Hero was to best Slammin' Sammy again in 1942 and yet again in 1946. Not to worry, Snead took the North and South in 1941, as well as 1949 and 1950. In 1947, Babe Didrikson Zaharias captured the Women's North and South Amateur Championship there, while Jack Nicklaus took the men's version twelve years later.[5]

In 1915, course architect Donald Ross said of Pinehurst, "Many of the greens have been relocated and the surroundings cunningly devised in dips and undulations, with bunkers and apparent natural divergence in contour, which puts a premium upon the proper shot."[6] One such cunningly devised hole is the second, a par 4, 441-yard confidence crusher. The crowned putting surface resembles an upside down saucer, causing all but the most perfectly placed shots to roll backwards off the green. Shades of miniature golf on the PGA tour!

Given the three holes on the three courses described above, it's perfectly understandable if one were to liken a golf ball to the word of God.

What?

How in the world can an inanimate object be likened to the source that animates all humanity? How can a ball weighing less than two ounces and measuring no less than 1.68 inches in diameter be akin to the teachings of Jesus, who overcame sin by his death and resurrection? Chances are that the only area in which a golf ball surpasses Jesus is in the number of dimples. The little white orb typically has in the neighborhood of 300 to 450 dimples, while the Son of God presumably has considerably less. For the answer to how one can liken a golf ball to the Bible, turn to the Gospel of Mark, where the evangelist relates one of Christ's many parables—a short story with a big lesson attached:

Chances are that the only area in which a golf ball surpasses Jesus is in the number of dimples.

> He began to teach them many things in parables, and in his teaching he said to them: "Listen! A sower went out to sow. And as he sowed, some seed fell on the path, and the birds came and ate it up. Other seed fell on rocky ground, where it did not have much soil, and it sprang up quickly, since it had no depth of soil. And when the sun rose, it was scorched; and since it had no root, it withered away. Other seed fell among thorns, and the thorns grew and choked it, and it yielded no grain. Other seed fell into good soil and brought forth grain, growing up and increasing and yielding thirty and sixty and a hundredfold." And he said, "Let anyone with ears to hear listen!"

> *When he was alone, those who were around him along with the twelve asked him about the parables…. And he said to them, "Do you not understand this parable? Then how will you understand all the parables? The sower sows the word. These are the ones on the path where the word is sown: when they hear, Satan immediately comes and takes away the word that is sown in them. And these are the ones sown on rocky ground: when they hear the word, they immediately receive it with joy. But they have no root, and endure only for a while; then, when trouble or persecution arises on account of the word, immediately they fall away. And others are those sown among the thorns: these are the ones who hear the word, but the cares of the world, and the lure of wealth, and the desire for other things come in and choke the word, and it yields nothing. And these are the ones sown on the good soil: they hear the word and accept it and bear fruit, thirty and sixty and a hundredfold* (Mark 4:2-10, 13-20).

Now as to how a golf ball is like the word of God, just think of this parable in light of the three previously mentioned second holes. Then imagine Jesus at the nineteenth hole of the Galilean Golf Club:

> He began to teach them many things in parables, and in his teaching he said to them: "Listen up! A duffer went out to golf. And as he hit off many second tees, some of his drives landed in thickets surrounding the elevated green at Prairie Dunes. Others landed in the deep waters of Lake Kadijah at Medinah, well short of the green, and the balls were lost forever. Or they found the bunker on the backside and were trapped in the sand. Still other shots landed on

the outer edge of the green of the second at Pinehurst No. 2, where they could not find purchase and rolled back down the sides. Yet some balls were well-struck and landed smack dab in the middle of the fairway and brought forth easy access to the greens. Or on the greens themselves they were well positioned near the hole. Now, those shots were rewarded, some with par, others with birdies, still others with eagles."

And he said again, "Listen up!"

When he was back in the clubhouse, those who were in his foursome asked him about the parable. He said to them, "Don't you guys get it? If you don't understand this story, then how are you going to understand the rest of them? The golf ball is the word. The ball hit into the thickets at Prairie Dunes is like those who hear the word but let the cares of the world, the lure of wealth and the desire for material goods choke the word. It's a wasted shot. The drives that landed in the drink at Medinah are like the word that's heard but soon forgotten and lost forever. The shots in the bunker are like the word that's received but can't always be lived by. It may take a time or three to get back on course. Those shots that found the edge of the green at Pinehurst No. 2 are like the word that's well received at first, but soon those folks backslide, even though they don't intend to. But the drives on the fairway or the greens, that's the word of God that is well struck and goes where it's intended. It leads to spiritual pars, birdies or eagles. Now do you understand?"

Yes, follow the little white ball and we might just find salvation.

# Church Pews and Trinities

On the western side of the Big Island of Hawaii, near Kona, atop the black lava fields spewed by the nearby volcano for which it is named, sits the Mauna Kea Golf Club, designed by the great course architect Robert Trent Jones, Sr. Natives to the Island are quick to point out that of the 13 recognized climates on the planet, 11 reside here, from the snow-capped flanks of the area's namesake volcano some 13,700 feet above the black sand beaches at sea level to the rain forest on the isle's northern most tip.[1] Few golf courses offer the beauty and diversity of Mauna Kea's view of snow-white volcano, rugged black lava beds and pristine blue ocean waters.

God's geography combines with Mr. Jones' artistry to create one of the most photographed of all golf holes in the world, the third at Mauna Kea. A crescent-moon shaped inlet, framed by the ever-present, pockmarked black lava, allows for surging surf to meet rocky shoreline with dramatic flair. Making the par 3, 261-yard hole even more spectacular is the fact that the ocean actually separates cliff-side tee from opposite cliff-side green. Should one be fortunate enough to carry over the sea, the biblical number of plenty—seven—awaits in the form of seven carefully placed bunkers that surround the green.

In 1892, The Country Club in Brookline, Massachusetts, became the nation's first country club. Two years later, the Club became one of the five charter members of what is now known at the United States Golf Association.[2] Keeping with this tradition of leadership, the club also played a part in ushering golf into America's mainstream consciousness. In 1913, Brookline hosted the U.S. Open that one of two renowned English golfers was expected to win. After all, Harry Vardon had captured one U.S. Open already, as well as four British Opens, and Ted Ray was the reigning British champ. Yet after 72 holes, the pair found themselves tied with a local lad by the name of Francis Ouimet. In a true story worthy of the best of national mythmaking, Ouimet had grown up across the street from the club and in his younger years worked there as a caddy. His familiarity with the course no doubt served him well as he won the 18-hole playoff, thrusting golf onto the front pages of sports sections everywhere.[3] In 1963, Julius Boros joined Ouimet as an Open winner at The Country Club, as did Curtis Strange 25 years later.[4]

The club's signature hole is its par 4, 444-yard third. With a dogleg to the right, the hole asks that you put your faith in your tee shot (and in God as the green cannot be spied from the elevated tee). Errant drives may find mounds or clusters of New England granite. At green site you find bunkers left and right, as well as a mound here and there. Situated on the outskirts of Boston, this may be Brookline's version of Bunker Hill. At the backside of the long, narrow green is a road and picturesque pond, where long irons often splash down. Though not a golfer, Tenley Albright used the frozen version of the pond to her advantage in preparing for the 1956 Winter Olympics, where she captured a gold medal in women's figure skating, this prior to her becoming a well-known surgeon and cancer expert.[5]

One of golf's most famous third holes is located at the Oakmont Country Club, just outside of Pittsburgh along the Allegheny River. First played in 1903, Oakmont is one of the country's noteworthy courses, having played host to a host of U.S. Open and PGA Championships. A list of victors includes a virtual "Who's Who" of golf: Gene Sarazen (1922 PGA), Bobby Jones (1925 U.S. Amateur), Sam Snead (1951 PGA), Ben Hogan (1953 Open), Jack Nicklaus (1962

Open) and Johnny Miller (1973 Open). Miller's final round of 63 is considered by many to be the greatest round of golf in the 20th century. More recently, Oakmont has toasted U.S. Open champions Ernie Els (1994) and Angel Cabrera (2007).[6]

What makes Oakmont's third so challenging is a series of berms or raised banks that straddle the third and fourth fairways. Called the Church Pews, these deep bunkers require a prayer to elude and, if you are caught among them, possibly a novena to escape. Perhaps taking a cue from the original apostles, the Pews count twelve. From the third tee to green, the Pews taper from front to back, measuring 43 yards at their widest to 18 yards at the narrowest, covering 102 yards in length total.[7] Picture a football field divided into berms. Making the sandy hazards all the more daunting is the fact that the fescue-thatched ridges are anywhere from three and a half to four feet tall. If in "church" at Oakmont, depending upon the lie, one may be forced to play backward or sideways rather than forward. Then again, after a few futile attempts at recovery, one may be tempted to just pick up the ball and go home.

But wait, there's more.

Beware of overcompensating to avoid the Pews on the left, because on the right of the narrow fairway are a series of five additional severe bunkers, cousins of the three that border the green. Father-son course designers Henry and William Fownes[8] must have felt enough was enough, for the third green, while elevated, is mostly flat, at least by Oakmont standards. Still, it does slope away from the golfer. Success at the third hole at Oakmont is a lot like success at life. Both need to be played straight and true. (By the way, having escaped the Church Pews on the left of the third fairway, golfers must face them again on the right of the fourth.)

Why call the berms at Oakmont the "Church Pews"? Why not the "Beach Benches" or the "Berm Bleachers"? Perhaps it has something to do with golf courses being analogous to places of worship. Golfers often plan their vacations around courses they wish to visit, traveling to the Big Island to play Mauna Kea and the Arnold Palmer-inspired Hapuna, to Hilton Head to challenge Harbour Town and Long Cove, to Monterrey to pay homage to Pebble Beach and Spyglass.

Dedicated linksters will cross the Atlantic for a chance to walk Saint Andrews or Carnoustie. Uber enthusiasts will plan to play during their lifetime the top hundred courses of the world as ranked by *GOLF Magazine*.

Baseball fans may never be able to throw off the mound at Yankee Stadium in New York or take batting practice at Safeco Field in Seattle. Football followers may not have the chance to kick a field goal at Soldier Field in Chicago or at the Los Angeles Coliseum. However, hitters of the small white ball can putt in the footsteps of Hogan and Snead at Pinehurst No. 2, British Open champions Gary Player and Tom Watson at Carnoustie, U. S. Open champion Tiger Woods at Bethpage Black, British Open winner Jack Nicklaus at Saint

Andrews, victorious Phil Mickelson at the TPC Sawgrass and more. A 20-handicapper from a local municipal course can stand where Palmer and Player, Nelson and Nicklaus, Hagen and Hogan, Sarazen and Snead, Jones and Miller, Watson and Trevino have all stood. And take in the history, lore and tradition of the great courses, players and championships.

The same can be said for God's faithful and churches.

Early churches became a repository for beautiful frescoes, statues and paintings depicting seminal moments in the history of Jesus and the saints. Until the advent of the printing press and the subsequent rise in literacy, art was the means of communication of biblical stories and faith traditions. Regions, towns, even neighborhoods built churches to be the center of religious, as well as social and political, life. Today, these monuments provide inspiration to those who visit them.

In Rome, for instance, there are more Catholic churches than days of the year. Members of the flock do indeed flock to Saint Peter's Basilica, one of the most recognized spiritual structures in the world and resident church for the pope since the 1600s. In 1976, I considered myself blessed to be able to participate in Christmas Mass at Saint Peter's as celebrated by Pope Paul VI. Other Christians visit San Pietro in Vincoli, which holds the chains that bound Peter in prison, as well as Michelangelo's imposing statue of Moses. Still others journey to Assisi where centuries-old churches contain relics of two of the most inspirational saints in Catholic history, Saint Francis and Saint Clare. Protestants visit beautiful historical churches in Wartburg, Zurich, London and Amsterdam.

With its rose windows, flying buttresses and twin towers, the

Cathedral of Notre Dame is one of the most visited sites in Paris, in France, in all of Europe. A John-Daly drive away is Sainte-Chapelle, with a veritable kaleidoscope of reds, golds, greens, blues and mauves from 15 glorious stained-glass windows portraying more than 1,000 religious scenes.[9] Entering these wonderfully holy buildings one feels honored, indeed, to be in God's house. There is a very similar feeling in visiting Oakmont's third and some of the other magnificent golf course holes around the world.

To visit such landmarks as these, both ecclesial and tee-able, is to share a spiritual and esthetic experience with millions who have done the same. There is a feeling of awe to be found amidst the Church Pews at Oakmont as there is to be discovered before the altar of the Cathedral of Notre Dame. Visits to the great golf courses of the world can increase our bonds to God and other golfers; pilgrimages to the venerable churches of the world can strengthen our relationship with God and the rest of the faithful.

Just as hole number three at Oakmont suggests a relationship between courses and cathedrals, the number three itself has a profound connection to both the game and God. In fact, attempting to master golf is akin to trying to grasp one of the most mysterious aspects of Christianity—the Blessed Trinity. That is to say, both are near impossible.

Golf represents a symbiotic relationship among golfer, ball and course. In fact this threesome is inextricably linked. Take away one of the three elements and the game of golf ceases to be. What's more, professional golfers are often defined by what they do with the golf ball on a particular course at a particular moment in history.

For example, Arnold Palmer has become part of the lore of Cherry Hills for his aggressive play in the 1960 U.S. Open. His four straight birdies on the final day propelled him to the championship. There's even a plaque at the first hole at Cherry Hills to commemorate "Arnie's Charge." On the lighter side, Palmer and Cherry Hills are also connected off the course. For it was there that he ordered the heretofore unheard of combination of iced tea and lemonade, thereby concocting the drink that bears his name—the Arnold Palmer![10]

Johnny Miller goes golf-gloved hand in hand with Oakmont by virtue of his amazing final round 63 en route to the 1973 U.S. Open title. Tiger Woods announced that he had the golf world by the tail when he won his first major championship at Augusta, capturing the 1997 Masters, setting a four-round record of 18 under par while doing so.

Jack Nicklaus will be forever linked with Muirfield in Scotland. Having won the British Open there in 1966, he repeated in 1980. The Golden Bear so loved his experiences at Muirfield that he chose it for the name of the Dublin, Ohio, course of his own design. As for the Black Knight, Gary Player, he is etched into the annals of Oakland Hills South in Bloomfield Hills, Michigan, for a spectacular iron shot on the sixteenth hole that led to his second PGA championship in 1972.

Mention good-natured Lee Trevino and Oak Hill in Rochester comes to mind, site of the first of his six major championships, the 1968 U.S. Open. Given Trevino's impoverished childhood, this was especially gratifying for the man known as the Merry Mex. With regard to "T" shots, T is for Tom Watson and Turnberry, Scotland, where in 1977 he shot back-to-back 65s to close with a British Open victory over rival Jack Nicklaus. Incidentally, Nicklaus was runner up to both Trevino and Watson four times each in golf's major tournaments, a testament to all three golfer's superior abilities.

Golfer, ball and course. Their mystical relationship calls to mind the interconnectedness of the Blessed Trinity, one of the most recognized and least understood concepts within the Christian faith. Simply put, the Holy (or Blessed) Trinity is three persons—Father, Son and Holy Spirit—in one God.

Far be it from me to try to explain in a few paragraphs what theologians have devoted the better part of two millennia trying to understand. Three distinct persons in the same one God is a mystery to be sure. But it is also a blessing. For in each of the three persons we have the opportunity to come to better know the one true God. In God the Father, we pray to the creator of all that is. Through God the Son, we are able to forge a relationship with Jesus who walked the earth and died for our sins. Through the Holy Spirit, comes our awareness of God and his love for us.

There are several references in scripture that reveal the unique relation of these persons to each other: *And Jesus came and said to them, "All authority in heaven and on earth has been given to me. Go therefore and make disciples of all nations, baptizing them in the name of the Father and of the Son and of the Holy Spirit"* (Matthew 28:18-19).

John's Gospel offers several insights into the Trinity. In one of the Good Book's most famous passages, Jesus states: *"For God so loved the world that he gave his only Son, so that everyone who believes in him may not perish but may have eternal life"* (John 3:16).

When John the Baptist baptized Jesus in the River Jordan, all three persons of the Trinity were present: *In those days Jesus came from Nazareth of Galilee and was baptized by John in the Jordan. And just as he was coming up out of the water, he saw the heavens torn apart and the Spirit descending like a dove on him. And a voice came from heaven, "You are my Son, the Beloved; with you I am well pleased"* (Mark 1:9-11).

Don't worry if you have trouble grasping the concept of the Blessed Trinity. After all, Jesus' own disciples, men who had been with him day in and day out hearing Christ teach and preach, did not fully understand: *Philip said to him, "Lord, show us the Father, and we will be satisfied." Jesus said to*  him, *"Have I been with you all this time, Philip, and you still do not know me? Whoever has seen me has seen the Father. How can you say, 'Show us the Father'? Do you not believe that I am in the Father and the Father is in me? The words that I say to you I do not speak on my own; but the Father who dwells in me does his works. Believe me that I am in the Father and the Father is in me; but if you do not, then believe me because of the works themselves"* (John 14:8-11).

There are times in our lives when each person of the Trinity offers us the best gateway to God. At the birth of a child, for example, ecstatic parents thank creator God profusely for the miracle they hold in their hands. At times of temptation or frustration, we may pray to Jesus for the strength to endure the human journey, knowing that

Christ faced most of the same experiences we do. When seeking how to best serve God with the talents he has given us, we seek guidance from the Spirit. In each case we converse with a distinct person of the Trinity at the same time we forge a relationship with God.

To begin to understand the Trinity, think back to the relationship between the golfer, course and dimpled white ball. All three are linked. Remove one and there is no game of golf to play. As for Father, Son and Spirit, they too are inseparable. But instead of providing a mere game to play, the Blessed Trinity offers the faithful three distinct ways to relate to the one, almighty, eternal God.

Which is why the Three in One is even better than a hole in one.

# Grand Slams and Gospels

"Arrrgh!" (To be said with a patch over your eye and a parrot on your shoulder.) Thank Robert Louis Stevenson for the inspiration behind the names of the 18 holes at Spyglass Hill at Pebble Beach. And thank course architect Robert Trent Jones, Sr., for their design. As its name of the fourth hole suggests, Blind Pew does not offer a clear view of the green from the tee. One must negotiate a short dogleg to the left to fully observe the pin. Yet, one needs to know where said pin is placed in order to utilize the downhill fairway to the best advantage. If the pin is back, approaching from the right hand side of the fairway is preferred. If front, the left side offers a more favorable approach. The good news is there are no bunkers surrounding this par 4, 370-yard hole. The bad news is the Blind Pew doesn't need them. After all, the green is ringed by ice plant, sand and scrub. And if these don't affect how the hole is played, the stiff ocean winds often do.

On to Long Island, New York, for yet another difficult fourth, this one the par 5, 528-yarder at Bethpage Black in Farmingdale. Midway on the fairway, ruining what had been a marvelous stretch of lawn, is a good-sized — um, make that a large, rather imposing — cross bunker, a familiar element of architect A.W. Tillinghast's courses. Because of the angle of the nicely sculptured but dangerous Glacier Bunker, a golfer is forced to choose between two difficult plays. Take the safer course in three strokes, combining a shorter drive with an iron and short pitch from the right. Or go for birdie with a long drive, requiring the longer second shot to clear yet another series of bunkers in front of the green. Decisions, decisions. Tiger Woods made enough of the right choices to capture the 2002 U.S. Open here. While he is known for wearing his traditional red golf shirt during the final round, Tiger also looked good in Bethpage Black.

Referring to aggressive shots, television announcers covering a tournament often speak of a player (Gary and others) "attacking" the course. Well, if a course is going to be attacked, shouldn't it defend itself? That is the thinking behind the par 3, 195-yard fourth hole at the National Golf Links of America in Southampton, also on Long Island. Modeled after the original redan-type hole of North Berwick West in Scotland, the fourth at National takes advantage of natural rolling topography and a fiendishly protected green. By definition, a "redan" is an arrow-shaped embankment forming part of a fortification. On this hole, those embankments are concave and filled with copious amounts of sand. Those about to tee off from the elevated green have an unobstructed view of what awaits. Opening shots must carry across a sloping valley to the green sitting atop a plateau. Easier written than done. Packed on the bank in front of the green is a ball-attracting sand trap, while to each side are formidable bunkers, some ten feet deep. Twenty-five feet above the base of the bunkers, the green itself is no piece of cake either. From the tee, it angles away from the line of play, right to left. Not only does it angle away, it does so at a slope. In fact, the difference between the highest and lowest points on the green is five feet. As if all this isn't bad enough, the space behind the green drops off precipitously.

In addition to number four holes, the number four is significant in both the game and in the Bible. On the links there are four major tournaments—Masters, U.S. Open, British Open and PGA Championship—that make up the Grand Slam of golf. The term was first used to describe four important tournaments won by Bobby Jones in 1930 (more on this at the Sixteenth Hole chapter). For today's Grand Slam, read on.

The (British) Open Championship began in 1860 at Prestwick in Scotland. Thirty-five years later, the U.S. version of the Open Championship was played at the Newport Country Club in Newport, Rhode Island. That tournament consisted of 36 holes played in a single day over a single nine-hole course.[1] Like the British Open and PGA Championship, the U.S. Open is played on different courses each year. Recent host courses have included Oakmont, Winged Foot West, Pinehurst No. 2, Shinnecock Hills, Bethpage Black, Southern Hills and Pebble Beach.

In 2008, one of the most exciting U.S. Opens ever was played at Torrey Pines Golf Club in La Jolla, California. After five days and 90 holes, Rocco Mediate and Tiger Woods were tied, thanks to Tiger's pressure-packed 2-foot birdie putt on the last hole of playoff play. Finally, on the 91st hole, in sudden death, Woods claimed victory by a single stroke. What made this victory for Woods so sweet—and remarkable—was that it came two months after arthroscopic surgery on his left knee. It also occurred without Woods playing in a single tournament prior to the Open to work out the kinks in his game. Adding even more lore to the legend, it was revealed that Woods played with a double stress fracture in his left leg, the tibia to be exact. Victory did not come without a price, however. Tiger was forced to miss the rest of the year to undergo reconstructive anterior cruciate ligament (ACL) surgery on his left knee.

These days, U.S. Open courses typically play longer than most tournaments, highlighted by pinched fairways, high rough and hilly greens. Played in mid-June, the U.S. Open schedules its final round to fall on Father's Day. It's a nice reminder to give thanks for fathers everywhere, including the one who is in heaven:

> *Our Father in heaven,*
> *hallowed be your name.*
> *Your kingdom come,*
> *Your will be done,*
> *on earth as it is in heaven.*
> *Give us this day our daily bread.*
> *And forgive us our debts,*
> *as we also have forgiven our debtors.*
> *And do not bring us to the time of trial,*
> *but rescue us from the evil one* (Matthew 6:8-13).

In 1916 the first PGA Championship was held in Bronxville, New York, at the Siwanoy Country Club. Winner Jim Barnes earned $500 for his efforts.[2] Compare that to the $1.26 million for 2007 PGA champ Tiger Woods.[3] Sponsored by the Professional Golf Association of America, the PGA Championship reserves 20 of its 156 places for club professionals, who qualify a month prior to the PGA, which is usually played in August four weeks after the British Open. Courses that have welcomed the PGA of late have included Southern Hills, Medinah, Baltusrol Lower, Oak Hill East, Hazeltine and Winged Foot West.

Played the second weekend in April, the Masters Tournament is held annually at Augusta National in Augusta, Georgia. Traditions include a course ablaze with the color of spring flowers, winners being fitted with green blazers, and members of the sport's storied past serving as starters. Ben Hogan, Gene Sarazen and Arnold Palmer have all been the first to tee off at hole number one to begin this fabled tournament. In 1934, Horton Smith won the first tournament played at Augusta, while Jack Nicklaus has worn the green jacket six times.[4]

Only five players have won a career Grand Slam[5]—that is, winning at least one each of the four major tournaments:

| Player | Masters | U.S. Open | British Open | PGA |
| --- | --- | --- | --- | --- |
| Jack Nicklaus | 6 | 4 | 3 | 5 |
| Tiger Woods | 4 | 3 | 3 | 4 |
| Ben Hogan | 2 | 4 | 1 | 2 |
| Gary Player | 3 | 1 | 3 | 2 |
| Gene Sarazen | 1 | 2 | 1 | 3 |

Both the Golden Bear and the Tiger have three career Grand Slams. Woods holds the distinction of holding the four championships simultaneously, though not in the same calendar year. He won the U.S. and British Opens and the PGA in 2000 and the Masters the following spring. This quartet has become known as the Simultaneous Slam. Not quite as catchy a term as Grand Slam, perhaps that's why the feat has also been called the Tiger Slam, a phrase with more teeth to it.

If the New Testament were to have a Grand Slam or a Tiger Slam, chances are it would be the four Gospels of Matthew, Mark, Luke and John. Each of these evangelists portrays the life of Jesus for their particular audience. Matthew's focus was to prove to Jewish readers that Jesus was the Messiah and promised King. In writing to Theophilus, a Gentile, Luke reassured his friend that Jesus' message of salvation was for Jews and Gentiles alike: *Since many have undertaken to set down an orderly account of the events that have been fulfilled among us, just as they were handed on to us by those who were eyewitnesses and servants of the word, I too decided, after investigating everything carefully from the very first, to write an orderly account for you, most excellent Theophilus, so that you may know the truth concerning the things about which you have been instructed* (Luke 1:1-4).

Luke is also credited with a sequel of sorts, the Acts of the Apostles (think of it as Luke II), which, as its name suggests, recounts the triumphs and tribulations of the early followers of Christ.

**John's account can be likened to playing the gorse and links of Scotland.**

The texts of Matthew, Mark and Luke are considered the "synoptic" gospels, in that they provide a general summary of Christ's life. Matthew and Luke take time to portray the early life of Jesus, as evidenced by the well-known nativity narratives. Their versions are like a long par 5, with lots of elements building on one another. Mark, on the other hand, plunges right in with Jesus' ministry, beginning with his baptism by John the Baptist in the River Jordan. The evangelist is concerned with the actions and accomplishments of the Lord. His story is more like a short par 3, played direct from tee to green.

John's Gospel is different than the others. If the synoptics are like playing American courses with lush fairways, John's account can be likened to playing the gorse and links of Scotland. It's a different experience, to be sure, but one just as challenging and wonderful. By presenting a strong case for Jesus' divine nature, John relates through Christ's signs and teachings how the Lord is savior of the world and how we all can be saved. Think of John as a book on how to perfect your swing, an indispensable guide to the 18 holes of life.

As to who were these scribes of Scripture, these chroniclers of Christ, the New Testament provides us clues, if not confirmed facts. Matthew, for instance, was either one of the original twelve apostles handpicked by Christ or perhaps one of Matthew's close followers. The former tax collector recounts the experience:

> As Jesus was walking along, he saw a man named Matthew sitting at the tax booth; and he said to him, "Follow me." And he got up and followed him.
>
> And as he sat at dinner in the house, many tax collectors and sinners came and were sitting with him and his disciples. When the Pharisees saw this, they said to his disciples, "Why does your teacher eat with tax collectors and sinners?" But when he heard this, he said, "Those who are well have no need of a physician, but those who are sick. Go and learn what this means, 'I desire mercy, not sacrifice.' For I have come to call not the righteous but sinners" (Matthew 9:9-13).

Paul refers to Mark in one of his epistles: *Aristarchus my fellow prisoner greets you, as does Mark the cousin of Barnabas* (Colossians 4:10). Luke corroborates the connection: *Then after completing their mission, Barnabas and Saul (Paul) returned to Jerusalem and brought with them John, whose other name was Mark* (Acts 12:25). It should be noted that

Barnabas was nominated to replace Judas as a member of the twelve apostles. Finally, Mark also traveled with Peter (1 Peter 5:13), the rock upon whom Christ chose to build his church. Being exposed to Peter, Paul, Barnabas and other leaders of the early church gave Mark a unique perspective on the foundations of Christianity. He may have even have had a first-hand view of the arrest of Jesus. His is the only gospel to record the presence of a youth on the scene, thought to be Mark himself: *A certain young man was following him, wearing nothing but a linen cloth. They caught hold of him, but he left the linen cloth and ran off naked* (Mark 14:50-52).

Mark's writing style can be likened to the interrogative style of Joe Friday of the old Dragnet TV series: "Just the facts, ma'am." Not wasting time, the evangelist establishes within his first few paragraphs the baptism of Jesus, his temptation by the Devil and the calling of the first disciples:

> *And just as he was coming out of the water, he saw the heavens torn apart and the Spirit descending like a dove on him. And a voice came down from heaven, "You are my Son, the Beloved; with you I am well pleased."*
>
> *And the Spirit immediately drove him out into the wilderness. He was in the wilderness forty days, tempted by Satan, and he was with the wild beasts; and angels waited on him....*
>
> *As Jesus passed along the Sea of Galilee, he saw Simon and his brother Andrew casting a net into the sea—for they were fishermen. And Jesus said to them, "Follow me and I will make you fish for people"* (Mark 1:10-13, 16-17).

In six short verses, Mark establishes Jesus' relationship within the Holy Trinity, his power over Satan, and the beginning of Christ's ministry. Talk about a spare writing style!

As for Luke's influences, he accompanied Paul on many of the latter's journeys, helping to spread the word to the fledgling Christian communities that were taking hold throughout the Mediterranean area. Luke retells of these experiences in his Acts of the Apostles, often writing of Paul and he as "we." In his own epistles, Paul refers to Luke: *Luke, the beloved physician, and Demas greet you* (Colossians 4:14) or *Only Luke is with me* (2 Timothy 4:11).

Like Matthew, John was probably one of the twelve, perhaps the youngest. As such he was present to many of the events in Jesus' life, partaking in conversation, gaining insight, intimately knowing the Son of Man, as Jesus called himself. In his Gospel, John refers to himself four times as "the one whom Jesus loved." He, along with his brother James and Peter, were often invited by Jesus to accompany him in moments of triumph or despair. The three witnessed the raising of the official's daughter from the dead, the Lord's agony in the garden the night before he died and, earlier, the Transfiguration: *Now about eight days after these sayings Jesus took with him Peter and John and James, and went up on the mountain to pray. And while he was praying, the appearance of his face changed, and his clothes became dazzling white. Suddenly they saw two men, Moses and Elijah, talking to him. They appeared in glory and were speaking about his departure, which he was about to accomplish at Jerusalem* (Luke 9:28-31).

John was also present at the foot of the cross when Jesus was crucified. There, the Lord entrusted his mother, Mary, to him, and him to her. No doubt Mary and John each learned from the other details about Jesus' life and ministry. To further add credence to his account, John closed his Gospel with the following: *This is the disciple who is testifying to these things and has written them, and we know that his testimony is true. But there are also many other things that Jesus did; if every one of them were written down, I suppose that the world itself could not contain the books that would be written* (John 21:24-25).

Just as golf has its recorded history, so too does the life of Jesus. Still, with sportswriters covering the game and evangelists writing of the Son of God, there are pieces that are missing. For instance, no one is certain who designed the old course at Saint Andrews, perhaps the most venerated 18 holes in the world. Similarly, little is told of Jesus' childhood. From the approximate ages of 12 to 30, his life seems to be a blank slate. As John mentions at the close of his Gospel, there were countless other events in Christ's life that took place that went undocumented. Though we don't know everything about the links or the Lord, we'll see in subsequent holes that much can be gained from what has been passed on to us.

# Payne Stewart and Palm Sunday

Said Davis Love III about the Colonial Country Club in Fort Worth: "This is the best, most traditional course without an ocean we play every year." Lanny Wadkins added, "It's a pure ball-striker's course. It's one of the finest classic courses we'll ever get to play." Then again, the great Ben Hogan opined, "A straight ball will get you in more trouble at the Colonial than any course I know."[1]

One of the holes that a straight ball will get you into trouble on is the par 5, 472-yard fifth, the third of the three holes that make up the Horrible Horseshoe. At first glance, it's a gentle dogleg to the right. However, this dog's leg has plenty of bite. Trees line both sides of the narrow landing area. Beside these arboreal sentries on the left hand side is a ditch, while further down the right hand side is a water hazard in the form of the Trinity River, named after the Father, Son and Holy Spirit. Avoid these and you have just enough time to take a deep breath before facing a circular green bordered by sand traps at two, four and eight o'clock. Put another way, this is a good time to be ever so accurate with your short game.

Quite possibly the toughest par 4 in the country is the 483-yard fifth hole at Pinehurst No. 2. Few par 4s cover this much distance. Only the 490-yard tenth at Augusta immediately comes to mind. What makes the Pinehurst fifth so challenging is that the second shot, typically a mid-iron, must be hit with the ball above a player's feet, thanks to the uphill slope of the wide landing area. Then, course designer Donald Ross' slightly elevated green represents a bogey or worse waiting to happen. Like a caddy carrying clubs in the heat, it has sloping shoulders. Even its "sweet spot" is beset with ripples in the greenscape. Of course to hit the green, one must avoid the bunkers on either side. Most shots from the fairway miss their mark, resulting in the need for a fantastic chip shot followed by an amazing putt, a combination not many have at their disposal.

Founded by a soda fountain magnate and first played in the late 1890s, Pinehurst hosted a major tournament in 1936 with the PGA Championship, won by Denny Shute.[2] New Zealander Michael Campbell captured the U.S. Open in 2005 on course No. 2, as did Payne Stewart six years before. Stewart's victory points out one of the many valuable lessons contained in, yes, the Bible.

Known for his colorful outfits—plaid pants and tam o'shanter caps paying and playing tribute to golfing attire of yesteryear—Payne Stewart first burst upon the major scene with his victory in the 1989 PGA Championship at Kemper Lakes in Illinois. Two years later, he followed up with a U.S. Open win at Hazeltine in Minnesota. In 1999, U.S. Open championship number two came on Pinehurst No. 2. Only a few months later, with his career in full swing, Stewart met a sudden and unfortunate demise. While traveling from Orlando to Dallas for a year-end tournament, Stewart died of hypoxia—lack of oxygen—when the private jet in which he was flying suffered a gradual loss of cabin pressure killing all six on board. Stewart was only 42 years old.[3] The golfing and sporting world was stunned. As tragic and unexpected as his death was, Stewart's passing reminds golfers and non-golfers everywhere of Jesus' warning about our tenuous ties to this life: *"But about that day or hour no one knows, neither the angels in heaven, nor the Son, but only the Father. Beware, keep alert; for you do not know when the time will come. It is like a man going on a journey, when he leaves home and*

*puts his slaves in charge, each with his work, and commands the doorkeeper to be on the watch. Therefore, keep awake—for you do not know when the master of the house will come, in the evening, or at midnight, or at cockcrow, or at dawn, or else he may find you asleep when he comes suddenly. And what I say to you I say to all: Keep awake"* (Mark 13:32-37).

No one knows the day or the hour when we will be called home: *"Keep awake therefore, for you do not know on what day your Lord is coming. But understand this: if the owner of the house had known in what part of the night the thief was coming, he would have stayed awake and would not have let his house be broken into. Therefore you also must be ready, for the Son of Man is coming at an unexpected hour"* (Matthew 24:42-44).

Will we be worthy of the room our Father has prepared for us? That all depends on how well we've lived our lives, the sorrow in our hearts for our own failings, and the forgiveness we have offered to others. Just as every new hole in golf is an opportunity for redemption from a previous one poorly played, every new day offers a chance to right our lives. As to how we should do this, Matthew relates a pertinent story:

*Then someone came to him and said, "Teacher, what good deed must I do to have eternal life?" And he said to him, "Why do you ask me about what is good? There is only one who is good. If you wish to enter into life, keep the commandments." He said to him, "Which ones?"*

*And Jesus said, "You shall not murder; You shall not commit adultery; You shall not steal; You shall not bear false witness; Honor your father and mother; also, You shall love your neighbor as yourself." The young man said to him, "I have kept all these; what do I still lack?" Jesus said to him, "If you wish to be perfect, go, sell your possessions, and give the money to the poor, and you will have treasure in heaven; then come, follow me." When the young man heard this word, he went away grieving, for he had many possessions (Matthew 19:16-22).*

In this set of instructions from Jesus we learn it is not enough to just attend church services and abide by the Ten Commandments. We must also serve by contributing our time, treasure and talent to those in need. All too often, we find that our possessions actually possess

**All too often, we find that our possessions actually possess us.**

us. It may be a desire to own the latest in fashion season after season, to own the largest TV, fastest car or best set of clubs. We may fall into being possessed by our kids' busy schedules— driving them to school, piano lessons, the tutor, soccer, lacrosse, baseball, swimming, ballet, parties. None of these things is bad in and of themselves. Yet God has bestowed on us gifts not so we can accumulate as much as possible but rather share as much as we can: *"From everyone to whom much has been given, much will be required; and from the one to whom much has been entrusted, even more will be demanded"* (Luke 12:48).

Bethpage Black in New York presents another stern test with its own fifth hole, a par 4, 446-yard affair. From yet another elevated tee one must carry a hazard called by some a diagonal bunker, by most a vast wasteland. Avoiding the bunker only brings a golfer face to face with a group of handsome oak trees that some call a stand and others would classify as a small forest. At the end of the rolling fairway is a steep climb to the green, some 30 feet above. Consider it good fortune to be able to see the top of the pin from this deep spot. Saucer like in contour, the green is circled by a ring of thick grass and protected by an impressive sand trap in front and two brethren left and right. To take the fifth, one would do well to fade the first shot and draw the second. Either that or fade away completely.

Bethpage—spelled *Bethphage*—also makes an appearance in the Bible:

> *When they had come near Jerusalem and had reached Bethphage, at the Mount of Olives, Jesus sent two disciples, saying to them, "Go into the village ahead of you, and immediately you will find a donkey tied, and a colt with her; untie them and bring them to me. If anyone says anything to you, just say this, "The Lord needs them. And he will send them immediately." This took place to fulfill what had been spoken through the prophet, saying,*
>
> *"Tell the daughter of Zion, Look, your king is coming to you, humble, and mounted on a donkey, and on a colt, the foal of a donkey."*
>
> *The disciples went and did as Jesus had directed them; they brought the donkey and the colt, and put their cloaks on them, and he sat on them. A very large crowd spread their cloaks*

*on the road, and others cut branches from the trees and spread them on the road. The crowds that went ahead of him and that followed were shouting,*

*"Hosanna to the Son of David! Blessed is the one who comes in the name of the Lord! Hosanna in the highest heaven!"*

*When he entered Jerusalem, the whole city was in turmoil, asking, "Who is this?" The crowds were saying, "This is the prophet Jesus from Nazareth in Galilee"* (Matthew 21:1-11).

Christ's triumphant entrance into Jerusalem is commemorated every year on the Sunday before Easter. Known as Palm Sunday, the day is named for the palm leaves passed out to the congregation calling to mind the branches spread before Jesus as part of his procession into Jerusalem.

What makes this event significant in the gospels is that it represents the pinnacle of Jesus' time on earth from a secular or popular point of view. The Old Testament had long predicted the coming of a Messiah who would set the Jews free. A descendant of King David, this savior was expected to be, like the famous ancestral monarch, a military and political leader who would liberate the Jews from their oppressors, in this case the Roman Empire. Jesus was thought to be such a person. No wonder the Jews celebrated his arrival to the holy city.

Of course, any rebel who might upset the status quo was a threat to the Roman occupation. And any prophet thought to be the Messiah was also a threat to the Pharisees and Sadducees, the religious leaders of the day. Finally, anyone who upset financial matters, as Jesus did upon his arrival, was a threat to commerce:

*Then Jesus entered the temple and drove out all who were selling and buying in the temple, and he overturned the tables of the money changers and the seats of those who sold doves. He said to them, "It is written,*

*'My house shall be called a house of prayer; but you are making a den of robbers.'*

*The blind and the lame came to him in the temple, and he cured them. But when the chief priests and scribes saw the amazing things that he did, and heard the children crying out in the temple, "Hosanna to the Son of David," they became angry* (Matthew 21:12-15).

No wonder Jerusalem was in turmoil. Most of the world today knows what happened next. Within five days time, Jesus, the proclaimed Messiah, was crucified for supposedly claiming to be the King of the Jews. In most people's eyes, Jesus had gone from king to criminal, from the height of popularity to ignominy, from representing hope to being forgotten. Even Christ's own apostles and disciples were shaken in their beliefs: *It was evening on that day, the first day of the week, and the doors of the house where the disciples had met were locked for fear of the Jews* (John 20: 19).

How in the world, one might ask, could someone fall from such heights to such depths in just a few days? Believe it or not, the game of golf can provide a clue.

During the 1996 Masters, Australian Greg Norman tied the course record at Augusta National with a 63 in the opening round. With his long blonde, almost white, hair, Norman was known as the Great White Shark. His first-round tally prompted scores of interviews and hundreds of headlines. The Shark had taken a huge bite out of Augusta. Norman had mastered the Masters. He was, like Jesus, king for a day. Entering into the final round on Sunday, the Aussie had a commanding six-stroke lead. In one of the greatest folds in the game, however, Norman sputtered to a 78 while Nick Faldo took charge with a 67, winning the coveted green jacket by five strokes.[4] In three days, Norman had gone from sitting on top of the golfing world to being thought of in some circles as a loser, despite a remarkable career that included two British Open championships. Fortunately, the Shark was able to recover and is now swimming pretty. He's worth hundreds of millions of dollars and spends time among his business interests, which include golf course design and his own world-class wine label.[5]

Granted, Norman's fall and subsequent rise are but poor human analogies to something divine and mysterious. But each and every day, we must die to something old and rise to something new. A painful divorce gives way to a new life. Seeing children off to college offers parents the time to pursue their own interests. The loss of a job can provide the opportunity to pursue a passion. Life presents us with the opportunity for rebirth, if we are open to it.

As for Jesus, paradoxically his most devastating moment—his crucifixion—was the catalyst for his crowning glory. For on the third day, he rose from the dead, conquering sin and death in the process. By reconciling each one of us to his Father in heaven, Christ has opened the door for us to go home to our Father as well.

# Golf and Bethlehem

Less than an hour north of New York City are not one but two of the nation's most acclaimed golf courses: Winged Foot East and West. Located in Mamaroneck, the golf club takes its name from the fleet-footed Mercury[1]—Roman deity, herald and messenger of the gods. Among other things, Mercury is also god of eloquence and skill,[2] two words that come to play when golfers come to play Winged Foot.

First, eloquence. In the early 1920s, New York was already home to the National and Shinnecock Hills on Long Island, while neighboring New Jersey boasted of Baltusrol. Members of the New York Athletic Club desired a course that equaled if not surpassed those landmarks in every measure. Even today golfers and scribes alike speak persuasively of Winged Foot's beauty and challenge, which leads to skill. Given the rustic area with which he had to work, architect A.W. Tillinghast designed 36 holes that require an abundance of this particular attribute by any who play.

Over the years Winged Foot West has welcomed quite a few of golf's major championships to its fairways and greens. In 1929, none other than Bobby Jones captured the U.S. Open there. Three decades later Billy Casper was crowned Open champ. In 1974 and 1984, Hale Irwin and Fuzzy Zoeller outpaced their respective Open fields. More recently, the West course gave Davis Love III the love in the form of the 1997 PGA Championship. And in 2006, Geoff Ogilvie claimed his U.S. Open championship.

Winged Foot West will make an appearance at the Tenth Hole chapter. For now, attention is turned to the East Course, specifically hole number six, nicknamed Trouble[3] by the devious Mr. Tillinghast, for this par 3, 194-yard effort allows for plenty of it. This is true, especially at the raised green, where four shallow sand traps—or are they small beaches?—protect its manicured lawn.

For another really nasty course, travel to Angus, Scotland. There lie the links of Carnoustie. First played in the 1500s, the course is called by some "Car-nasty"[4] for its rather stern play and unwelcoming wind off the North Sea. A 19-year-old Sergio Garcia left the course in tears after carding an 89 and 83 during the 1999 British Open.[5] His bogey on the 18th during the 2007 version of the championship cast him in a four-hole playoff with eventual winner Pádraig Harrington, who double bogeyed the hole himself.[6] But for a sheer collapse of epic proportions, bordering on gallows humor, Frenchman Jean Van de Velde's name will live long in golfing infamy.

During that 1999 British Open, Van de Velde needed only a double bogey six on the final hole to add another V to his name (for victor). After a nondescript tee shot, the Frenchman managed to hit the upper tier of the grandstand with his second, the carom landing in the deep rough. Jean's third shot was not what it could have been, landing in the burn (water) for a penalty stroke. His next shot found the bunker on the right hand side of the green. Shot six at long last landed 10-feet from the cup, and shot seven finally found the hole for a triple bogey.[7] (This actually sounds like one of my better holes.) Eventually, Paul Lawrie won a playoff against Justin Leonard and Van de Velde, becoming the first Scotsman in nearly 70 years to win the British Open on native soil. To think Lawrie was ranked 159th in the world before the start of tournament play.[8] Lawrie's incredible win calls to mind a familiar verse from Matthew: *So the last will be first* (Matthew 20:16).

One of the nine courses in the rota or rotation for the British Open

Championship, Carnoustie is considered one of the most difficult, in part because of its sixth hole. The par 5, 578-yard effort has earned the sobriquet Long for obvious reasons. However, it just as easily could have been nicknamed Difficult, Demoralizing or Downright Depressing. Anywhere a ball is likely to land there are deep bunkers, a winding, water-filled ditch called Jockie's Burn, and a post and wire fence along the entire left hand side from tee past green. Oh, there's also a sand trap behind the green, hidden from view from the fairway. To the mind's eye the deep bunkers midway down the fairway and in front of the green resemble giant footprints of a massive prehistoric mastodon. No wonder the course is called The Beast.[9] It was on the sixth at the 1968 Open that Jack Nicklaus landed his drive on the wrong side of the seemingly innocent-looking fence, costing him a two-stroke penalty. As fate would have it, the penalty pair happened to be the difference between his final score and that of Gary Player, who claimed the championship.

Finally, a book on golf and the Bible wouldn't be complete without a visit to Bethlehem—Pennsylvania that is–and the Saucon Valley Country Club Old. In a state that counts Merion and Oakmont among its offerings, Saucon Valley Old can hold its eighteen holes up proud. Its sixth hole many golfers find particularly vexing. Framed by magnificent trees, the fairway doglegs right. It's at this juncture that care must be taken for the second shot needs to carry over an expanse of scrub and sand reminiscent of Pine Valley in New Jersey, giving the hole its name: Sahara. Placement is critical, too, for trees bordering the right hand side block the approach to that patch of green the flagstick calls home.

For a brief moment in time, Bethlehem—Judea that is—was called home by the Holy Family:

> *Now the birth of Jesus the Messiah took place in this way. When his mother Mary had been engaged to Joseph, but before they lived together, she was found to be with child from the Holy Spirit. Her husband Joseph, being a righteous man and unwilling to expose her to public disgrace, planned to dismiss her quietly. But just when he had resolved to do this, an angel of the Lord appeared to him in a dream and said, "Joseph, son of David, do not be afraid to take Mary as your wife, for the child conceived in her is from the Holy Spirit. She will bear a son, and you are to name him Jesus, for he will save his people from their sins." All this took place to fulfill what had been spoken by the Lord through the prophet:*
>
> *"Look, the virgin shall conceive and bear a son, and they shall name him 'Emmanuel,' which means, 'God is with us.'"*
> *When Joseph awoke from sleep, he did as the angel of the Lord commanded him; he took her as his wife, but had no marital relations with her until she had borne a son; and he named him Jesus* (Matthew 1:18-25).

One might think that the savior of the world might be welcomed into being with pomp and circumstance. Not so, as Luke relates: *In those days a decree went out from Emperor Augustus that all the world should be registered. This was the first registration and was taken while Quirinius was governor of Syria. All went to their own towns to be registered. Joseph also went from the town of Nazareth in Galilee to Judea, to the city of David called Bethlehem, because he was descended from the house and family of*

*David. He went to be registered with Mary, to whom he was engaged and
who was expecting a child. While they were there, the time came for her to
deliver her child. And she gave birth to her firstborn son and wrapped him
in bands of cloth, and laid him in a manger, because there was no place for
them in the inn* (Luke 2:1-7).

A manger. Typically found in a barn. Mary and Joseph shared a
bed of straw with common farm animals, hardly the circumstances to
greet the son of the Most
High who had created
the entire universe, who
has dominion over all
living things, who is
not confined by time or
space. Yet, here it was
that God graced our
world as an infant, born
to modest parents in a
most unbecoming locale.

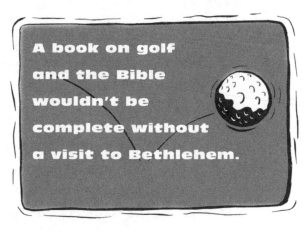

A book on golf
and the Bible
wouldn't be
complete without
a visit to Bethlehem.

And just because Jesus walked our earth was no guarantee that
we on earth would welcome him:

> *In the time of King Herod, after Jesus was born in
> Bethlehem of Judea, wise men from the East came to Jerusalem,
> asking, "Where is the child who has been born king of the Jews?
> For we observed his star at its rising, and have come to pay him
> homage." When King Herod heard this, he was frightened, and
> all Jerusalem with him; and calling together all the chief priests
> and scribes of the people, he inquired of them where the Messiah*

*was to be born. They told him, "In Bethlehem of Judea...."*

*Then Herod secretly called for the wise men and learned from them the exact time when the star had appeared. Then he sent them to Bethlehem, saying, "Go and search for the child; and when you have found him, bring me word so that I may also go and pay him homage."...And having been warned in a dream not to return to Herod, they left for their own country by another road.*

*When Herod saw that he had been tricked by the wise men, he was infuriated, and he sent and killed all the children in and around Bethlehem who were two years old or under, according to the time that he had learned from the wise men* (Matthew 2:1-5, 7-8, 12, 16).

During the Christmas holidays, Christians the world over celebrate the birth of Jesus in Bethlehem. Hymns are sung. Pageants are performed. Stories are told of how angels appeared to shepherds in the field saying: *"Glory to God in the highest heaven, and on earth peace among those whom he favors!"* (Luke 2:14).

However, Jesus was born in the most humbling of settings. What's worse, almost immediately he had a bounty on his head. Not the most promising of starts for the Son of God. But out of such beginnings great things may come.

Take Lee Trevino.

Born in 1939 into poverty in Texas, Lee Trevino never knew his father. Cared for by his grandparents, the young boy worked the cotton fields at age five to help the family earn money. As a youngster, an uncle gave him a few old golf balls and a rusty club and his love affair with golf began. After eighth grade, Trevino had to leave school in order to work. He began to caddy at a local course, earning money as well as being allowed valuable practice time on the course. As a seventeen-year-old he joined the Marine Corps and served for four years. Not long after his discharge, he joined the PGA tour. In 1968, his second year on tour, Sergeant Trevino captured the U.S. Open at Oak Hill and never looked back. Another four major tournament victories—the 1971 U.S. Open, the 1971 and 1972 British Opens, and the 1974 PGA—earned Trevino the sobriquet Super Mex. In 1984 he had added a PGA Championship at the age of forty-four.[10]

Impoverished. Cotton fields. Eighth grade education. Caddy. Self taught. Not quite the pedigree one would expect of one of the greatest golfers of his time. Perhaps it's not so hard then to imagine a young baby being born in a manger some 2000 years ago overcoming threats on his life to teach, preach and redeem the world.

# The Number of Plenty

Amber waves of grain describe America the beautiful—as well as the Sand Hills Club in Mullen, Nebraska. In the mid 1990s, Ben Crenshaw and Bill Coore purchased 8,000 acres amidst the rolling hills and sandy dunes 70 miles north of North Platte, with the express purpose of creating a world-class links-style course on American soil. Though called Sand Hills, the area was quite fertile in terms of possibilities for holes. Crenshaw and Coore found 130 sites, which they narrowed down to the final eighteen.[1] The overall effect is one of endless beauty punctuated in green. One thinks less of covering the course in golf carts than in covered wagons.

One particular hole captures the essence of Sand Hills: the seventh. At 283 yards, the hole is short for a par 4. Yet what it lacks in length it makes up for in cunning. For starters, what gives all that amber grain its poetic waves is the prairie wind. A soft breeze produces a gentle motion of the grasses that resembles the rolling hills on which grain grows. A stiff gale lays the grasses flat and wreaks havoc with drives and irons, even putts. Wind and direction can cause even the most meteorological of golfers to take pause. Mental calculations ensue as to placement of shot versus length. Landing on the lawn in two becomes paramount as the narrow patch of green, amidst grain as far as the eye can see, has an eight-foot deep bunker on its left hand side, sure to add a stroke or two to wayward shots. Shading to the right of the green is no sure thing either, as there is sharp drop off to a small valley below. In either case one marvels over the Crenshaw/Coore course work amidst God's handiwork.

On the banks of the Genesee River in upstate New York lies the Oak Hill Country Club in Rochester, a truly beautiful area of the country, especially during fall foliage season. Site of multiple U.S. Opens and PGA Championships, Oak Hill counts some of the game's most recognizable names among its victors: Walter Hagen (1934 Open), Dr. Cary Middlehoff (1956 Open), Lee Trevino (1968 Open), Jack Nicklaus (1980 PGA) and Curtis Strange (1989 Open).

One of its signature holes, principally designed by Donald Ross, is the par 4, 461-yard seventh. Two factors combine to provide a driver's test of the golfing variety. At approximately 22 yards across, and bordered by walls of trees, the fairway is quite narrow. What's more, there is a creek running diagonally across the landing area, forcing ball strikers to make a decision: play long and to the left of the fairway or short and to the right. Should one decide on the former and mistakenly shade right, water could be in the future as well as a sight line beset with nearby trees. If the latter strategy is employed, a longer approach to the green is required, running the risk of encountering one of two bunkers forward of the green. Either way, two precise shots are required to make the green, where those who arrive safely face another two to make par.

One of the most famous seventh holes in the world resides on the California coast at the Pebble Beach Links Course on Monterrey Bay. A par 3, 106-yard hole sounds innocent enough, unless its entire right hand and back sides are bordered by the pounding surf of the Pacific Ocean. Fair weather, the birdies come out; wind and/or rain, and the bogeyman or worse awaits. This is due to the large J-shaped trap in front of the green, a thick horseshoe-shaped one on the left, and four other smaller ones at the rear. Now, sand around greens is nothing new. However, when the green is small and the wind is blowing, traps and sea become much more diabolical forces with which to deal.

So just how small is the green at the seventh at Pebble Beach? Try 2,000 square feet in size and eight yards across at its narrowest point.[2]

When the green is small and the wind is blowing, traps and sea become much more diabolical forces.

Sand Hills, Oak Hill and Pebble Beach are but three of the seventh holes that try men's (and women's) souls. Just as easily mentioned could have been the A.W. Tillinghast-designed seventh at the San Francisco Country Club, the Robert Trent Jones-inspired challenge at the Olympic Club in the same city, or the Jack Nicklaus-created seventh hole at Grand Cypress in Orlando. For that matter, any of the more than 32,000 number seven holes around the world would have served us well.

Seven is also the number of plenty in the Bible. There are seven days in the creation narrative in the Book of Genesis. The Book of Revelation alone could be considered "seven heaven," with references to seven churches, seven golden lamp stands, seven stars, seven Spirits of God, seven lamps of fire, seven seals, seven angels who stand before God, seven trumpets, seven thunders, a red dragon having seven heads, a beast of the sea having seven heads, seven bowls and seven plagues. And the Gospel of Matthew records that seven loaves were used to feed the four-thousand: *Then Jesus called his disciples to him and said, "I have compassion for the crowd, because*

*they have been with me now for three days and have nothing to eat; and I do not want to send them away hungry, for they might faint on the way. The disciples said to him, "Where are we to get enough bread in the desert to feed so great a crowd?" Jesus asked them, "How many loaves have you?" They said, "Seven, and a few small fish." Then ordering the crowd to sit on the ground, he took the seven loaves and the fish; and after giving thanks he broke them and gave them to the disciples, and the disciples gave them to the crowds. And all of them ate and were filled* (Matthew 15:32-37).

In the Christian tradition, the number seven plays a significant role. There are lists the seven gifts of the Holy Spirit: wisdom to judge all things as God sees them; understanding with deeper insight the truths God has revealed to us; right judgment to act with prudence; courage to do great things for God; knowledge to see the things of the world in their relation to God; piety to love God as our Father and to have affection for all persons and things; and a fear of the Lord, of offending and being separated from him whom we love.[3]

Seven also covers everything from sins to sacraments. The former are of the capital, or deadly variety: anger, covetousness, envy, gluttony, lust, pride and sloth; the latter are much more full of grace: baptism, reconciliation, Eucharist, confirmation, marriage, holy orders, and the sacrament of the sick.

Perhaps the most important mention of the abundance associated with the number seven has to do with the forgiveness of sins. At the risk of condensing a good part of the New Testament into a single sentence, Jesus, the Son of God, was born of Mary, preached, taught, was crucified, died and was buried, only to rise three days later, thereby conquering sin and death, and showing us the way home to God the Father. Three of Christ's most important and recurring teachings were love of one another, service to others and the forgiveness of sins. Regarding the latter, Jesus spoke often: *"Do not judge, and you will not be judged; do not condemn, and you will not be condemned. Forgive, and you will be forgiven; give and it will be given to you. A good measure, pressed down, shaken together, running over, will be put into your lap; for the measure you give will be the measure you get back"* (Luke 6:37-38).

In Matthew's Gospel, the evangelist recounts how Jesus used a multiple of the number seven to reinforce his point: *Then Peter came and said to him, "Lord, if another member of the church sins against me, how often should I forgive? As many as seven times? Jesus said to him, Not seven times, but, I tell you, seventy-seven times"* (Matthew 18:21-22).

Given that seven represented abundance in Scripture, Peter must have thought he was being more than generous in his tolerance of his fellow followers. But to Jesus, even numerous times of forgiveness was not enough. Christ's reply of "seventy-seven times" could be likened to the modern day mathematical equivalent of "infinity plus one." Now, that's a lot of forgiveness! So important was this notion that Jesus reiterated his message to the disciples upon visiting with them after his death and resurrection:

*When it was evening on that day, the first day of the week, and the doors of the house where the disciples had met were locked for fear of the Jews, Jesus came and stood among them and said…. "Peace be with you. As the Father has sent me, so I send you" When he said this, he breathed on them and said to them, "Receive the Holy Spirit. If you forgive the sins of any, they are forgiven them; if you retain the sins of any, they are retained"* (John 20:19, 21-23).

*Then he said to them, "These are my words that I spoke to you while I was still with you—that everything written about me in the law of Moses, the prophets and the psalms must be fulfilled." Then he opened their minds to understand the scriptures, and he said to them, "Thus it is written, that the Messiah is to suffer and to rise from the dead on the third day, and that repentance and forgiveness of sins is to be proclaimed in his name to all nations* (Luke 24:44-47).

Who would have thought that the seventh hole in golf could help proclaim the forgiveness of sins?

# Claret Jug, Cup of Wine

Southeast of Traverse City, Michigan, on the western edge of the state, is the town of Frankfort. There, perched on a bluff overlooking Lake Michigan and the much smaller Crystal Lake is the Crystal Downs Country Club. In the 2000 census, Frankfort had less than 2,000 people, yet it has one of the best golf courses in the country. Crystal owes its grand design to none other than course architect Alister MacKenzie, he of Augusta, Cypress Point and Royal Melbourne fame. Of all his courses, one of Mr. MacKenzie's most signature holes is the eighth here in the upper reaches of Lower Michigan.

A 550-yard par 5 might draw notice just from sheer length alone. However, it's the topography of the hole that makes it unique. Picture a throw rug on a freshly waxed hardwood floor. Now take a running start and slide on that rectangle of carpet. The resulting rows of ridges, each with a rolling peak and valley, represent the contours in miniature of this standout hole. Enlarge it, cover it with fairway and call it the eighth at Crystal.

Key to playing the hole successfully is to position the second shot on the right hand side of the fairway near the right rough, where it will have a flatter lie. Land on the left and your resulting second stroke must be struck from an awkward stance in an uphill position. Complicating matters is that such a shot is often blind to the uphill green. Speaking of which, that verdant patch of real estate presents its own problems. It, too, is rolling, perched as it is on the top of a small hill. Shots that don't carry the green run the risk of catching the uphill fairway, only to roll some 40 yards backwards down the fairway, sinister compliments of the design firm of Gravity and MacKenzie.

After successfully playing the seventh hole at Pebble Beach, or

losing two sleeves of balls in the process, one has little time to relax
for the eighth awaits. Any 416-yard par 4 crossing a coastal chasm is
certain to make even the most confident golfers a little less so. Those
adverse to risk play the hole as a dogleg right. Those more daring, a
group whose number goes down when the wind comes up, launch
their second shot from the elevated landing area and across an inlet
of the Pacific, a chasm of 180 yards.[1] Oceanic water hazard aside,
the green offers its own
problems, with a ring
of three bunkers and
a slope front to back.
When playing Pebble
Beach, golfers often
reach for three items in
this order: prayer book,
camera and, finally, their
club of choice.

If Sand Hills requires a
covered wagon
to negotiate,
Troon may very
well demand an all-
terrain vehicle.

Small greens everywhere owe their existence to the eighth hole
at Royal Troon in Ayrshire, Scotland. Founded in 1878, Troon is one
of the nine courses in the rotation of the British Open Championship.
This cross-Atlantic major has received the royal treatment at Troon
eight times, with such notables as Arnold Palmer (1962), Tom Weiskopf
(1973), Tom Watson (1982) and Justin Leonard (1997) claiming the
Claret Jug given the winner.

Royal Troon is a collection of dunes, links, bumps and hollows.
If Sand Hills requires a covered wagon to negotiate, Troon may very
well demand an all-terrain vehicle. At 129 yards, the par 3 eighth
is the shortest hole of all in the British Open rotation. While short,

it's big on challenges. Known the golfing world over as The Postage Stamp,[2] it's not difficult to see why. From an elevated tee, one must loft an iron over a gulley onto the long but extremely narrow green— only 25 feet in width. Size, or lack thereof, of putting surface is not the only concern. Most always, wind plays a factor at the Open, as does the terrain. A large dune on the left protects the green from the wind, making gusts harder to read. Guarding the green on the left are two bunkers, while a large crater bunker shields the approach. On the right, errant shots inevitably find one of two deep bunkers with near vertical faces. Simply put, the tee shot must reach the green. If not, chances are no amount of postage will be able to cover the quantity of shots one will need for the ball to reach its destination.

Those who prevail at the British Open Championship at Royal Troon, Muirfield, Carnoustie, Saint Andrews or any of the courses that make up the Open rota (or rotation) receive the coveted Claret Jug as a symbol of their victory. When Young Tom Morris won the Open for the third time in a row, he became the outright owner of the Challenge Belt, the first Open prize. Thus, in 1872 a new award— the Claret Jug—came into being.[3] Inscribed The Golf Championship Trophy, the original resides at the Royal and Ancient Golf Club of Saint Andrews. The current jug was first awarded in 1928 to Walter Hagen and has the name of every Open champion inscribed. Winners are presented with this version of the jug, but must return it before the next year's Open, receiving a replica in its place.

English great Harry Vardon holds the record for most British Opens won with six (1896, 1898, 1899, 1903, 1911, 1914). Scotland's James Braid captured the championship five times (1901, 1905, 1906, 1908, 1910), as did American Tom Watson (1975, 1977, 1980, 1982, 1983).

Other notable multiple winners include American Walter Hagen, South African Bobby Locke and Australian Peter Thomson with four wins apiece, and Jack Nicklaus, Tiger Woods and Englishman Nick Faldo with a trio of jugs to their credit. Remarkably, Thomson was victorious three years running (1954-56) and four out of five years in a row, with the 1957 crown going to Locke.

As for why it is called the Claret Jug, the British have been fond of the wine for centuries. What the French call Bordeaux, the English call claret, a term that's been around for more than 300 years. Claret has also come to mean a shade of red resembling the color of the wine. It's also English slang for blood, with giving a bloody nose known as "tapping the claret."[4]

Wine and blood also were instrumental in the Lord's ministry as recorded in the New Testament. A reluctant Jesus began his ministry when his mother made a simple request concerning the fruit of the vine:

> On the third day there was a wedding in Cana of Galilee, and the mother of Jesus was there. Jesus and his disciples had also been invited to the wedding. When the wine gave out, the mother of Jesus said to him, "They have no wine." And Jesus said to her, "Woman, what concern is that to you and to me? My hour has not yet come." His mother said to the servants, "Do whatever he tells you."
>
> Now standing there were six stone water jars for the Jewish rites of purification, each holding twenty or thirty gallons. Jesus said to them, "Fill the jars with water." And they filled them up

*to the brim. He said to them, "Now draw some out, and take it to the chief steward." So they took it. When the steward tasted the water that had become wine, and did not know where it came from (though the servants who had drawn the water knew), the steward called the bridegroom and said to him, "Everyone serves the good wine first, and then the inferior wine after the guests have become drunk. But you have kept the good wine until now."*

*Jesus did this, the first of his signs in Cana of Galilee, and revealed his glory; and his disciples believed in him* (John 2: 1-11).

Whether claret was served that day, no one knows. What is certain is that figuratively and literally, wine played an important part in Jesus' teaching: *"I am the true vine, and my Father is the vinegrower. He removes every branch in me that bears no fruit. Every branch that bears fruit he prunes to make it bear more fruit. You have already been cleansed by the word that I have spoken to you. Abide in me as I abide in you. Just as the branch cannot bear fruit by itself unless it abides in the vine, neither can you unless you abide in me. I am the vine, you are the branches. Those who abide in me and I in them bear much fruit, because apart from me you can do nothing. Whoever does not abide in me is thrown away like a branch and withers; such branches are gathered, thrown into the fire, and burned. If you abide in me, and my words abide in you, ask for whatever you wish and it will be done for you"* (John 15:1-8).

Jesus' statement—*"I am the vine, you are the branches"*—is one of the most memorable in the Bible. Most Christians realize that we are all offshoots of the vine, that the Lord is the root of our faith. Apart from Christ we are nothing. We may face trials and tribulations in our lives. These may be what Jesus had in mind when he said that the Father "prunes" those branches that bear fruit so that they may bear even more. At times our faith is tested by the loss of a loved one, the ravages of disease, the destruction of our home by natural disaster, a child lost to addiction, a son or daughter killed in service to our country. We realize that we don't have all the answers. Despite our resources, we can't do it all. Indeed, without Jesus our vine and the Father our vine-grower we are nothing. Our faith is tested so we may become even stronger in faith.

What may be not as well known or, more accurately, conveniently forgotten within these verses is that those apart from the Lord face an unenviable existence. Hints are made about the fires of hell (more on this in future holes). Fortunately, Jesus tells us all we need to know to bear fruit: abide by and follow his commandments. And what might those commandments be?

Jesus told Peter to *"Feed my sheep"* (John 21:17). When faced with the hungry multitude, Christ said to the apostles, *"You give them something to eat"* (Luke 9:13).

To the rich man he said, *"You know the commandments: 'You shall not murder; You shall not commit adultery; You shall not steal; You shall not bear false witness; You shall not defraud; Honor your father and mother'.... Go, sell what you own, and give the money to the poor, and you will have treasure in heaven."* (Mark 10:19, 21).

Jesus, by his very example, shows us that we are to do good works as well. We are to serve our fellow human beings, on bended knee if necessary:

*Jesus poured water into a basin and began to wash the disciples' feet and to wipe them with the towel that was tied around him. He came to Simon Peter, who said to him, "Lord, are you going to wash my feet?" Jesus answered, "You do not know now what I am doing, but later you will understand." Peter said to him, "You will never wash my feet." Jesus said to him, "Unless I wash you, you have no share with me." Simon Peter said to him, "Lord, not my feet only but also my hands and my head!"*

*"Do you know what I have done to you? You call me Teacher and Lord—and you are right, for that is what I am. So if I, your Lord and Teacher, have washed your feet, you also ought to wash one another's feet. For I have set you an example, that you also should do as I have done to you…. If you know these things, you are blessed if you do them"* (John 13:5-9, 12-15, 17).

If Jesus can humble himself at the feet of his disciples, surely so can we. And how might we do that? Jesus provides that answer as well: *"For I was hungry and you gave me food, I was thirsty and you gave me something to drink, I was a stranger and you welcomed me, I was naked and you gave me clothing, I was sick and you took care of me, I was in prison and you visited me"* (Matthew 25:35-36).

From Hurricane victims in New Orleans to earthquake survivors in Pakistan, from AIDS sufferers in Africa to refugees of the war-torn Sudan, the world offers ample opportunities to feed, clothe and comfort those in need. After all, we have had an exemplary teacher: *"Truly I tell you, just as you did it to one of the least of these who are members of my family, you did it to me"* (Matthew 25:40).

All of this is prelude to one of the most precious gifts Jesus gave us: His body and blood to be shared with us in the forms of bread and wine: *Then he took a cup, and after giving thanks he said, "Take and divide it among yourselves; for I tell you that from now on I will not drink of the fruit of the vine until the kingdom of God comes." Then he took a loaf of bread, and when he had given thanks, he broke it and gave it to them, saying, "This is my body, which is given for you. Do this in remembrance of me." And he did the same with the cup after supper, saying, "This cup that is poured out for you is the new covenant in my blood"* (Luke 22:17-20).

Inscribed on the Claret Jug is the name of every winner of the British Open, proof positive that the likes of Vardon, Watson, Hagen and others will be with us in memory. Every time the Last Supper is recalled or reenacted by Christians, we receive a sacred reminder that God is, indeed, with us.

# Learn at the Turn

Yale University—home of Presidents Taft, Bush, Clinton and Bush—
is also the home of a world-class golf course, ingeniously named the
Yale Golf Course. While the course's name holds no surprises, many
of its holes most definitely do. Take number nine for instance. This
211-yard par 3 gem begins from a tee 60 feet above Greist Pond, a
body of water that spans nearly 200 yards to the green on the far side.
New England woods surround the still waters. In short, the scene
is a picture of serenity itself, disturbed only by the sound of under-
hit golf balls plopping into the pond. Twelve feet above the distant
bank is one of the more interesting greens in the country. Sixty yards
from front to back would suggest a spacious landing area. However,
dividing the green in two happens to be a depression, gully, trench
some five to eight feet deep. Land on the wrong side and any chance
of par goes down the drain, so to speak.

Going from Yale to Yale Bowl is not a matter of finding the
football field. It involves a trip from New Haven in Connecticut to East
Hampton on Long Island. Known for the National and Shinnecock
Hills, Long Island is also home to The Maidstone Club, a wonderful
display of links designed on American soil. Its ninth is a 400-yard par
4 with a view of the Atlantic from the raised tee. Dunes left and right
catch any wind-blown drives, though those landing in the tall grass
on the port side may never be seen again. At 370 yards, a large sand
ridge cuts across the fairway to bedevil anyone who tries to hit large
and go for the green. Yale Bowl, a ten-foot-deep natural bunker rests
to the right of the green, ready to gobble up any errant iron shots.
Once on the putting surface, the wind may again interfere with any
balls rolling toward the hole. With wind, bunker, bowl, dunes, grass,

ice plant and cypress trees, this maid is anything but genteel.

On the west coast, Captain Smollett also offers a challenge on nine. That would be Captain Smollett[1] of the Spyglass Hill Smolletts. This par 4, 431-yard uphill affair has a slight angle to the right, though playing that line runs the risk of encountering a sand trap halfway to the flagstick. Tall, leafy sentinels from tee to green guard the left hand side. Fortunately, the green is quite large, bordering on humungous; unfortunately, two deep bunkers protect it. If the uphill fairway doesn't provide a stern enough test, the sloping back-to-front putting sanctuary will.

When you are playing the first or front nine holes on a golf course, you are considered "going out," that is away from the home of the clubhouse. Conversely, when playing the last or back nine holes, players are considered to be "coming in," heading back to the nineteenth hole. When you end the ninth, you are said to be "at the turn." At this halfway point of our round (book actually), a look to certain terms common to both the game of golf and the Good Book might be appropriate.

**Eagle:** To those blessed with a long, accurate drive or an unerring putt, a score of two under par for any hole is called an eagle.

In the Old Testament, the Book of Exodus tells the story of how Moses delivered the Israelites out of captivity of Egypt to the Promised Land. Along the way, he visited Mount Sinai and received a covenantal message from God himself. An eagle figures prominently in the imagery: *Then Moses went up to God; the Lord called to him from the mountain saying, "Thus you shall say to the house of Jacob, and tell the*

*Israelites: You have seen what I did to the Egyptians, and how I bore you on eagles' wings and brought you to myself. Now therefore, if you obey my voice and keep my covenant, you shall be my treasured possession out of all the peoples. Indeed, the whole earth is mine, but you shall be for me a priestly kingdom and a holy nation* (Exodus 19:3-6).

From Exodus we learn what a wonderful feeling it is to know that we will be delivered to our Father on eagles' wings. The book of the prophet Isaiah has a similar reference: *But those who wait for the Lord shall renew their strength, they shall mount up with wings like eagles, they shall run and not be weary, they shall walk and shall not faint* (Isaiah 40:31).

How often has an eagle renewed the strength of a golfer's spirits, helping to spark a run of birdies to charge back into contention? So, too, can an eagle lift the believer's spirits to soar to the heavens.

**Green:** Each golf course has eighteen of these finely mowed patches of lawn—sometimes sloped, as number nine at Spyglass, or with a trench in the middle, as the ninth at Yale. Each green contains the hole in which the golf ball must ultimately come to rest.

In the Old Testament, the Book of Psalms is a collection of 150 poems written as songs to be sung in praise, lament, petition or thanksgiving. Most of them are attributed to King David, ancestor of Jesus. One of the most beautiful and comforting of all is Psalm 23, presented here in its entirety, including a most wonderful reference to a "green":

*The Lord is my shepherd, I shall not want.*
*He makes me lie down in green pastures;*
*he leads me beside still waters; he restores my soul.*

*He leads me in right paths for his name's sake.*
*Even though I walk through the darkest valley, I fear no evil;*
*for you are with me; your rod and your staff—they comfort me.*
*You prepare a table before me in the presence of my enemies;*
*You anoint my head with oil; my cup overflows.*
*Surely goodness and mercy shall follow me all the days of my life,*
*and I shall dwell in the house of the Lord my whole life long*
(Psalm 23).

It's the goal of most golfers to be "up" and "down" on a hole, meaning to chip up onto the green with one stroke and, with a

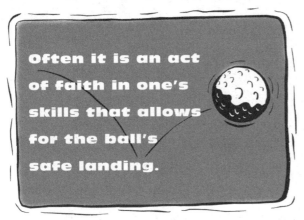

Often it is an act of faith in one's skills that allows for the ball's safe landing.

favorable lie, putt the ball down into the hole on the next. In other words, *to lie down in green pastures.* How comforting to a player to be able to do that with regularity. How much more comforting in life is it to know that no matter how much adversity we might face, the Lord is with us every step of the way, all the days of our lives.

**Blind:** Such a shot does not allow a golfer to see where the ball might land. Especially hilly courses, as well as those with sharp doglegs, have blind spots. Often it is an act of faith in one's skills that allows for the ball's safe landing.

On four different occasions in the gospels Jesus heals the blind as a demonstration of his power over sight. As on the golf course, when facing a blind shot, faith plays an important part as well: *As he approached Jericho, a blind man was sitting by the roadside begging. When he heard a crowd going by, he asked what was happening. They told him, "Jesus of Nazareth is passing by." Then he shouted, "Jesus, Son of David, have mercy on me…!" Jesus…asked him, "What do you want me to do for you?" He said, "Lord, let me see again." Jesus said, "Receive your sight; your faith has saved you"* (Luke 18:35-38,40-42).

**Carry:** This term refers to the distance between the playing and landing of a ball. Should a shot need to travel over a lake, river, Scottish burn, ocean inlet or, as at number nine at Yale, a pond to land safely, it will have to "carry the water."

In the days of Jesus, towns had a central well that provided water for the community. People, women mostly, had to go to the well with empty vessels, draw water, and "carry the water" home. In one such town on one such occasion, Jesus found opportunity to speak of spiritual drink: *A Samaritan woman came to draw water, and Jesus said to her, "Give me a drink." (His disciples had gone to the city to buy food.) The Samaritan woman said to him, "How is that you, a Jew, ask a drink of me, a woman of Samaria?" (Jews do not share things with Samaritans.) Jesus answered her, "If you knew the gift of God, and who it is that is saying to you, 'Give me a drink,' you would have asked him, and he would have given you living water." The woman said to him, "Sir, you have no bucket, and the well is deep. Where do you get the living water? Are you greater than our ancestor Jacob, who gave us the well, and with his sons and flocks drank from it?" Jesus said to her, "Everyone who drinks of this water will be thirsty again, but those who drink the water that I will give them will never be thirsty. The water that I will give them will become in them a spring of water gushing up to eternal life"* (John 4:7-14).

A word about Jews and Samaritans: In their day they got along about as well as the Palestinians and Jews do today. That's what made the lesson of the Good Samaritan so striking. What's more, a woman would not normally converse with a strange man. So in this passage, Jesus turns convention on its ear. By way of the Samaritan woman, he invites non-Jews to hear the word of God. Not just any non-Jews either, but those considered former enemies of Judea. Christ's invitation to the woman to partake in his spiritual drink is the equivalent to offering non-Jews—and therefore all non-chosen ones—eternal life. On the golf course, those who carry the water are that much closer to the Promised Land of the green. Thanks to a woman who chose to carry the water, we are all that much closer to the Promised Land of our Father's house.

**Caddy:** An invaluable companion on the golf course, a caddy carries a players clubs and offers sage advice on how to play difficult holes, club selection in certain situations, and the idiosyncrasies of the course. Wouldn't it be wonderful if we all had such a guide in life? Ah, but we do: *When the day of Pentecost had come, they were all together in one place. And suddenly from heaven there came a sound like the rush of a violent wind, and it filled the entire house where they were sitting. Divided tongues, as of fire, appeared among them, and a tongue rested on each of them. All of them were filled with the Holy Spirit and began to speak with other languages, as the Spirit gave them ability* (Acts 2:1-4).

God, working in the person of the Holy Spirit, gives us the guidance and moral compass to live a life worthy of life everlasting. It is through discernment—a process of imagining which of certain choices allow us to best do God's will—that the Spirit helps shape our lives. While it is often difficult to grasp the concept of the Blessed Trinity, here's a tip for the third person: Think of the Holy Spirit as the ultimate caddy.

**Holes:** On each green is a hole holding a cup into which the ball must land for the player to advance to the next hole. In the pages that follow, much drama will be recreated concerning wondrous shots made into key holes of major golf tournaments.

Holes also have a dramatic role in Bible:

> *But Thomas (who was called the Twin), one of the twelve, was not with them when Jesus came. So the other disciples told him, "We have seen the Lord." But he said to them, "Unless I see the mark (hole) of the nails in his hands, and put my finger in the mark of the nails and my hand in his side, I will not believe."*
>
> *A week later his disciples were again in the house, and Thomas was with them. Although the doors were shut, Jesus came and stood with them and said, "Peace be with you." Then he said to Thomas, "Put your finger here and see my hands. Reach out your hand into my side. Do not doubt but believe. Thomas answered, "My Lord and my God!" Jesus said to him, "Have you believed because you have seen me? Blessed are those who have not seen and yet have come to believe"* (John 20:24-29).

Using Thomas as an example, the Lord is reassuring the rest of us who have had moments of doubts in faith that Jesus realizes how hard it is at times to believe. However, he is with us after all. As Christ says: *"Do not fear. Only believe"* (Luke 8:50).

TENTH HOLE
# The Pulpit

Having made the turn, here we are on the back nine, with the first stop being sunny southern California. Located in the Santa Monica Canyon at the base of the like-named mountains in Pacific Palisades is the Riviera Country Club. George C. Thomas, architect of the neighboring Bel-Air Country Club, agreed to bring the Los Angeles Riviera to life, but only if he was granted carte blanche. Thus, at its completion in 1927 at a cost of $243,827.63, the Riviera was the second-most expensive 18-hole layout in the world.[1] While staggering at the time, this amount would not even make a divot in the purse of a tournament winner today.

Thomas created 15 designs for the course before arriving at his final choice. No less an authority than Alister MacKenzie proclaimed the site "was as fine as any he'd seen" and that the course was "as nearly perfect as man could make it."[2] This being southern California in the late 1920s, early enthusiasts at the course included Douglas Fairbanks and Mary Pickford. Home to the Los Angeles (now the Nissan) Open, Riviera is also known as Hogan's Alley, for the way Ben Hogan ruled the course. He captured three Los Angeles Opens as well as the 1948 U.S. Open there. Riviera also feted Hal Sutton and Steve Elkington at the 1983 and 1995 PGA Championships, respectively.

At 315 yards, the 10th at Riviera is a risk-reward par 4. Those about to tee off imagine birdies yet often leave with bogeys. Strategically placed, two bunkers intrude upon the fairway, one at 210 yards on the right, the other 45 yards further on the left. Players who learn from their mistakes choose between carrying the shorter of the two or laying up on the more distant fairway, hoping to avoid the thick rough. Those whose eyes are bigger than their club-heads may decide to try to drive the green, only to learn of its unforgiving slope from right to left or to find themselves among several small southern California beach-sized traps that protect the verdant dance floor.

On the opposite end of the country is, many would argue, one of the finest golf courses in the country, if not the world. Pine Valley Golf Club in Clementon, New Jersey, offers golfers test after test on hole after hole. Par is an achievement well earned, not easily gained. The very nickname of the seventh hole conjures up extremely difficult play: Hell's Half Acre.[3] George Crump and Harry Colt conceived eighteen unique combinations of green, grass, scrub, bunkers, topography and guile. A Who's Who of golf course architects have visited, and in some cases contributed to, the Pine Valley mystique, including Messrs. Fownes, MacDonald, MacKenzie, Thomas, Tillinghast and Ross.[4]

Considered one of the most difficult holes to play in the world, the tenth at Pine Valley is a short hole that's long on problems. This par 3, 146-yarder requires a perfectly placed iron to an undulating green that falls steeply to a deep bunker in front or coarse wastelands all around. Those unfortunate to land in the angled front bunker will find that the only way to play is to go back from whence they came. No doubt this particular feature has greatly influenced the hole's nickname:[5] the Devil's A__hole (um, well a portion of anatomy usually not discussed at fine dinner parties).

Move from New Jersey to New York and go from the Devil to the Pulpit[6] in the process. A.W. Tillinghast considered the tenth at Winged Foot the finest par three he ever designed,[7] this from the man who built Baltusrol Lower and Upper, Bethpage Black, Brook Hollow in Dallas, The San Francisco Golf Club, and Somerset Hills in

Bernardsville, New Jersey.

A 190-yard par 3, the Pulpit is the only hole on the West course of Winged Foot oriented east to west. All others run north and south, which means that one must adapt to a new wind direction at the beginning of the back nine. This is critical because an errant iron off the tee and one runs into trouble, which starts with T which rhymes with P which stands for Pulpit (as well as Panic). Miss long and a golfer runs the risk of landing in the trees behind the green or, worse, landing beyond the white stakes out of bounds. Miss left and one might encounter more trees that hug that side of the pear-shaped green or the bunker

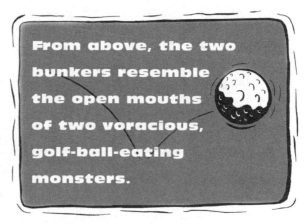

From above, the two bunkers resemble the open mouths of two voracious, golf-ball-eating monsters.

in front. Miss right and there's a bunker the size of which 1963 U.S. Open winner Julius Boros likened to a national park.[8] From above, the two bunkers resemble the open mouths of two voracious, golf-ball-eating monsters, both with an epiglottis of lawn protruding from the back of their "throats."

Should one be ever so fortunate to escape bunkers, trees and out of bounds, there is the putting surface itself with which to contend at the Pulpit. There are greens that slope...and there are greens that SLOPE. The West's tenth could double as a ski jump in the winter. The rear corners of the green are raised six feet higher than the front. Those who may gloat at having escaped danger with their tee shot may have only postponed their misery. For any putt tapped aggressively from the rear of the green is just as likely to roll downhill and find a bunker as it is the bottom of the hole. As on Sunday mornings in some churches, the lessons from the Pulpit can be quite severe.

As gentlemanly a game as golf is, with its rich traditions of the ocean links in Scotland and green blazers at Augusta, the sport has more than its fair, or fairway's, share of references to the netherworld. Both Pine Valley's seventh and number fourteen at Baltimore Country Club have been called Hell's Half Acre.[9] At Pine Valley, it's because a near 100-yard Sahara divides the fairway of this 580-yard par five. Sand, scrub and desert grass are surrounded by more sand, scrub and desert grass. This stretch of land nearly the length of a football field is more desert than sand trap. Should one's ball land here, forego the golf cart and continue on camelback for your next shot. Baltimore features a set of bunkers at the top of a hill on the uphill par 5, 603-yard hole. A misplayed ball on the fourteenth has just as much chance landing atop the hill in one of the bunkers or down in the adjacent gully. I guess making a birdie on either hole is like trying to escape Hades on your own.

Pine Valley's tenth is protected by the above-mentioned devilish bunker. And at this book's Hole 14, a visit will be paid to a bunker at Saint Andrews that is also named after the "home" of Lucifer.

In golf, being in one of these "hells" is a miserable experience, requiring far too many attempts to extricate oneself from such a place. No one wants to be there. In fact, most do everything they can to avoid such circumstance. Still, it happens, even to the best of golfers, the most skillful of ball strikers. Fortunately, a golfer can be released from hell, even if by virtue of playing another ball elsewhere. Not so in the real thing. To understand the inescapable fires of hell one need turn no further than the Bible.

As inspirational, holy and sacred as the Bible is, it most definitely has its seamier side. Evil abounds. No sooner has God created paradise than Satan in the form of the serpent is there to undermine the Almighty's creation: *Now the serpent was more crafty than any other wild animal that the Lord God had made. He said to the woman, "Did God say, 'You shall not eat from any tree in the garden?'" The woman said to the serpent, "We may eat of the fruit of the trees in the garden; but God said, 'You shall not eat of the fruit of the tree that is in the middle of the garden, nor shall you touch it, or you shall die.'" But the serpent said to the woman, "You will not die; for God knows that when you eat of it your eyes will be opened, and you will be like God, knowing good and evil." So when the woman saw that the tree was good for food, and that it was a delight to the eyes, and that the tree was to be desired to make one wise, she took of its fruit and ate; and she also gave some to her husband, who was with her, and he ate. Then the eyes of both were opened, and they knew they were naked; and they sewed fig leaves together and made loincloths for themselves* (Genesis 3:1-7).

Most know what happened next. Literally and figuratively, all hell broke loose:

> *The Lord God said to the serpent, "Because you have done this, cursed are you among all animals and among all wild creatures; upon your belly you shall go, and dust you shall eat all the days of your life...."*
>
> *To the woman he said: "I will greatly increase your pangs*

*in childbearing; in pain you shall bring forth children, yet your desire shall be for your husband, and he shall rule over you."*

*And to the man he said, "Because you have listened to the voice of your wife, and have eaten of the tree about which I commanded you, 'You shall not eat of it',' cursed is the ground because of you; in toil you shall eat of it all the days of your life; thorns and thistles it shall bring forth for you; and you shall eat the plants of the field.*

*By the sweat of your face you shall eat bread until you return to the ground, for out of it you were taken; you are dust, and to dust you shall return"* (Genesis 3:14, 16-19).

To the author of Genesis, the temptation in the garden was his way of saying that evil has been part of human existence from the beginning. And when God handed Moses the list of basic rules of human behavior, guess how many there were? Ten. (So it's no wonder that the tenth hole in golf is often a killer.)

The Book of Revelation, ascribed to Saint John of Patmos, has its own version how evil came to earth: *And war broke out in heaven; Michael and his angels fought against the dragon. The dragon and his angels fought back, but they were defeated, and there was no longer any place for them in heaven. The great dragon was thrown down, that ancient serpent, who is called the Devil and Satan, the deceiver of the whole world—he was thrown down to the earth, and his angels were thrown down with him* (Revelation 12:7-9).

Scripture certainly has its dark side. Cain murdered Abel. Jacob deceived Isaac. Moses killed an Egyptian overseer. David sent a solider to die in battle so he could bed the officer's wife. Herod had all the male children under two years old living near Bethlehem murdered. John the Baptist was decapitated. Judas Iscariot sold out Jesus for thirty pieces of silver. Even Jesus faced temptation by an evil spirit in the desert.

Jesus, full of the Holy Spirit, returned from the Jordan and was led by the Spirit in the wilderness, where for forty days he was tempted by the devil. He ate nothing at all during those days, and when they were over, he was famished. The devil said to him, "If you are the Son of God, command this stone to become a loaf of bread." Jesus answered him, "It is written, 'One does not live by bread alone.'"

Then the devil led him up and showed him in an instant all the kingdoms of the world. And the devil said to him, "To you I will give their glory and all this authority; for it has been given over to me, and I give it to anyone I please. If you, then, will worship me, it will be all yours." Jesus answered him, "It is written,

'Worship the Lord your God, and serve only him.'"

Then the devil took him to Jerusalem, and placed him on the pinnacle of the temple, saying to him, "If you are the Son of God, throw yourself down from here, for it is written,

'He will command his angels concerning you, to protect you,' and 'On their hands they will bear you up, so that you will not dash your foot against the stone.'"

Jesus answered him, "It is said, 'Do not put the Lord your God to the test,'" When the devil had finished every test, he departed from him until an opportune time (Luke 4:1-13).

The serpent tempted Eve. Satan tried to do the same to Jesus. Even though the unscrupulous one failed, he departed to wait for another, a better, a more opportune time. Evil exists. As for fires of hell, Jesus made reference to those himself: *If your hand or your foot causes you to stumble, cut if off and throw it away; it is better for you to enter life maimed or lame than to have two hands or two feet and to be thrown into the eternal fire. And if your eye causes you to stumble, tear it out and throw it away; it is better for you to enter life with one eye than to have two eyes and be thrown into the hell of fire* (Matthew 18:8-9).

Jesus does not ask us to maim ourselves. He exaggerates to make a point that we should eliminate whatever gets in the way of our relationship with the Father. In today's culture stumbling blocks come in the form of addiction, selfishness, materialism, vanity, ego, infidelity, lust and more. Even playing eighteen holes on Sunday rather than attending church services is a sin, if you can believe it. Just as the stumbling blocks are very real so too is the concept of hell.

While no one knows if the fires of hell actually exist, there is certainly an unworldly pain associated with the underworld. Our purpose in life is to be in right relationship with God, to find our way back home to our Father. To fail to do this is to be in a personal hell. After betraying Jesus, Judas Iscariot fell victim to the despair that comes from being out of favor with the Father: *When Judas his betrayer, saw that Jesus was condemned, he repented and brought back the thirty pieces of silver to the chief priests and elders. He said, "I have sinned by betraying innocent blood." But they said, "What is that to us? See to it yourself." Throwing down the pieces of silver in the temple, he departed; and he went and hanged himself* (Matthew 27:3-5).

A sad but true fact is that many of us, at some point of our lives, will face what Saint John Chrysostom called the "dark night of the soul." It is a feeling of utter hopelessness and helplessness. Perhaps the dark night comes swiftly as with the sudden, unexpected death of a loved one, or with the shocking news or a diagnosis of cancer. Maybe darkness arrives slowly as with gradual realization that one is addicted to drugs or alcohol. It could be a crisis of faith caused by the seemingly endless deaths due to violence, disease and disaster, or finding out that one is no longer valued as a working professional or as a spouse.

Any of these events or more can cause pain and anguish. Inconsolable grief eats away at the soul. The shock of terrible news numbs the mind. Loss of a loved one closes the heart. Depression sets in, followed by despair. Eating becomes difficult, sleeping impossible, even breathing can hurt. The cumulative effect is utter and total devastation of the spirit and the will to live. Nothing seems to ease the agony or stop the downward spiral into the depths of darkness. This then is hell on

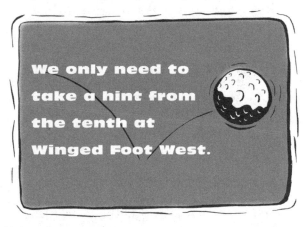

We only need to take a hint from the tenth at Winged Foot West.

earth, an excruciating searing of our heart and soul. Now imagine this feeling for all of eternity. Imagine being without hope, without consolation, without comfort. In short, without God's love. This then is the meaning of hell.

Needless to say, this is an experience none of us want to endure. As to how to avoid the road to perdition, we only need to take a hint from the tenth at Winged Foot West: Listen to the Lord at the pulpit. Wherever Jesus found himself he discovered a place to preach and teach about how to live our lives in right relationship with God and each other. He spoke to the woman at the well, the Syro-Phoenician woman, the Roman Centurion, the Jewish official. In other words, he talked with anyone who would listen: Jews and Gentiles, Roman oppressors and Temple officials, prostitutes and tax collectors.

One such pulpit was the Mount of Olives: *When the Son of Man comes in his glory, and all the angels with him, then he will sit on the throne of his glory. All the nations will be gathered before him, and he will separate people from one another as a shepherd separates the sheep from the goats, and he will put the sheep at his right hand and the goats at this left. Then the king will say to those at his right hand, 'Come, you that are blessed by my Father, inherit the kingdom prepared for you from the foundation of the world* (Matthew 25:31-34).

Quite often, the disciples were confounded by Jesus' words, no doubt summing up the same thoughts that go through anyone's mind digesting all of the above: *When the disciples heard this, the were greatly astounded and said, "Then who can be saved?"* (Matthew 19:25).

Fortunately, Jesus had the answer that they and we long to hear: *But Jesus looked at them and said, "For mortals it is impossible, but for God all things are possible"* (Matthew 19:26).

So while the road is narrow, the spirit is willing but the body weak, and it is easier for a camel to pass through the eye of a needle than for a rich person to gain heaven—there is always hope. Instead of the endless dark nights of eternity, there is light: *Again, Jesus spoke to them saying, "I am the light of the world. Whoever follows me will never walk in darkness but will have the light of life* (John 8:12).

Hallelujah!

For those who need a shorthand version of what is asked of us, an easy-to-manage par 3 so to speak, Jesus provided that too. In fact, the Lord, in his infinite wisdom, knew that his flock might have a hard time remembering everything he said, so he invented the sound bite: *A lawyer asked him a question to test him. "Teacher, which commandment is the greatest?" He said to him, "You shall love the Lord your God with all your heart, and with all your soul, and with all your mind.' This is the greatest and first commandment. And a second is like it: 'You shall love your neighbor as yourself'"* (Matthew 22:36-39).

# Saint Andrew—Course and Man

Situated in Springfield Township, New Jersey, are two more of golf course architect A.W. Tillinghast's creations: Upper and Lower Baltusrol. Together the courses have hosted seven U.S. Opens and one PGA Championship. Among the Open victors was Willie Anderson, a Scotsman who won in 1903, the first of three such victories in a row and one of four overall. Lower Baltusrol, if not the course that Jack built, could be considered the one that Nicklaus conquered, having won the U.S. Open there in 1967 and again in 1980. More recently, Lee Janzen took home the 1993 Open title, while Phil Mickelson was crowned 2005 PGA Champion.

In 1936, Tony Manero bested the field and the Upper course to etch his name in the U.S. Open record books. Key to his success was a 12-foot birdie putt on the eleventh hole to spark a charge from four strokes back.[1] To do so, Manero had to deal with a severely sloping green, well protected by bunkers. Before his successful putt, he had to negotiate the first 435 yards of this par four. Two competing features influence shot selection here. At the edge of the right rough is a rather large oak tree, which obscures play from that side of the fairway. Attempting to avoid the oak, one may instead fall victim to a set of bunkers on the left. (Whether greed or seduction, trees or traps, life presents plenty of obstacles we must overcome along the way.)

Founded in 1892, Shinnecock Hills Golf Club in Southampton, Long Island, is one of the five charter members of the Amateur Golf Association of America, known today as the United State Golf Association. As one of the oldest courses in the country, and as one of the best-known links designs, Shinnecock has been home to four different U.S. Opens—in three different centuries. Winners have included James Foulis in 1896 and Corey Pavin 99 years later. Retief Goosen found relief in winning in 2004.

In 1986, during the final round, Raymond Floyd sunk an 18-foot birdie putt at Shinnecock's eleventh to propel him to his Open title.[2] Many ruefully consider this hole one of the shortest par fives in golf. That it's actually a 158-yard uphill par 3 only confirms its difficulty! In ideal conditions and with a perfectly placed iron, this is a wonderful one-shot to the green. However, if the wind has its way, golfers run the risk of hitting short or long off the tee. Short may very well introduce the player to one of four unfriendly bunkers. Long, on the other hand, places undue pressure on a recovery shot. Hit the second shot too hard and the ball will roll off the front of the green (see aforementioned bunkers). Hit it too soft and said ball will roll back down the steep slope behind of the green, coming to rest where one will be forced to recover all over again.

Arguably the most famous golf course in the world is the old course at Saint Andrews. Located in Fife, Scotland, the links are so ancient that the original designer is unknown, though credit can certainly be given to the Almighty for the lay of the land. There are records from 1552 indicating that the area of what is now Saint Andrews was "zoned" for rearing rabbits, shooting, and playing golf and futbol.[3] Further, documents show that in 1506 King James IV bought a set of clubs at the course.[4] (Which gives new meaning to the term finding a fourth to play. Or should that be a IVth?)

In its long and storied history, Saint Andrews has hosted the Open Championship a record 27 times. Winners include some of the sports most recognized names: Bobby Jones (1927), Sam Snead (1946), Jack Nicklaus (1970, 1978), Seve Ballesteros (1984), Nick Faldo (1990),

John Daly (1995) and Tiger Woods (2000, 2005).

The course can be played in either direction, with anti- or counter-clockwise being the prevalent choice today. Also, to allow the links to rest, the Old Course is closed most Sundays, except for the final rounds of the Open Championship and other select tournaments. Even more unusual is the fact that certain greens on the course share holes.[5] One such pairing is for the seventh and eleventh holes, allowing outgoing players to mingle with incoming players, a truly civilized feature on a course full of tradition.

As for the eleventh hole at Saint Andrews, though a short par 3, its 172 yards are fraught with danger. For one, there's the cavernous Hill Bunker on the left, not to be confused with an abandoned missile silo. Should you hit long, there's the Eden Estuary awaiting splashdown. The deep Strath Bunker and a large kidney bean-shaped sand trap present their own forms of torture to be avoided. Finally, there's the green itself, a rather sloped putting surface that often results in three putts alone. This hole single-handedly cost Gene Sarazen the 1933 Open. Thanks to a triple-bogey six, including three to exit the Hill, he lost to Denny Shute by a stroke.[6]

Saint Andrews draws at least two of its many traditions from Scripture. That the course "rests" on most Sundays can be traced to God resting on the seventh day after creating the world and all that is. Grass, green and gorse are allowed to recuperate and refresh in order to welcome the world of golf anew at the start of every week. In the hectic hustle and bustle that passes for living these days, we would be wise to take a lesson from these storied links as well as the story in Genesis. Come Sunday, rest and reflect. While watching Woods and Mickelson go head to head in the FedEx Challenge is nice, we should make time for God in addition to golf. After all, the Third Commandment states "Remember to keep holy the Sabbath day," not "Remember to keep your head down until well after your follow through," though for the Christian golfer both are important.

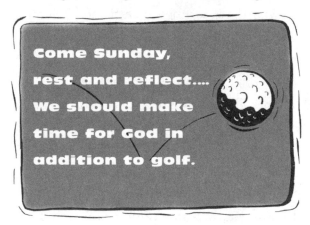

Come Sunday, rest and reflect.... We should make time for God in addition to golf.

That the course is named after a character from the Bible should come as no surprise. Saint Andrew is none other than Andrew, brother of Peter, one of the twelve apostles. While Peter, James and John get most of the ink in the Bible as far as the apostles go, Andrew, first a disciple of John the Baptist, may very well have been the first to realize Jesus was the Messiah:

> *The next day he (John the Baptist) saw Jesus coming toward him and declared, "Here is the Lamb of God who takes away the sin of the world...!" And John testified, "I saw the Spirit descending from heaven like a dove, and it remained on him. I myself did not know him, but the one who sent me to baptize with water said to me, 'He on whom you see the Spirit descend and remain is the one who baptizes with the Holy Spirit.' And I myself have seen and have testified that this is the Son of God."*
>
> *The next day John again was standing with two of his*

*disciples, and as he watched Jesus walk by, he exclaimed, "Look, here is the Lamb of God!" The two disciples heard him say this, and they followed Jesus. When Jesus turned and saw them following, he said to them, "What are you looking for?" They said to him, "Rabbi" (which translated means Teacher), "where are you staying?" He said to them, "Come and see...." One of the two who heard John speak and followed him was Andrew, Simon Peter's brother. He first found his brother Simon and said to him, "We have found the Messiah" (which translated means Anointed)* (John 1:29, 32-41).

What a wonderful exchange. Jesus asks Andrew, his unnamed colleague and by extension every one of us, "What are you looking for?" Good question. On a superficial level, we may be looking for a better car, nicer job, a bigger house, even the ability to drive a golf ball straight and far. On a deeper level, we seek security, comfort, love, the knowledge that our lives are meaningful and that there is more to life than death. "Where are you staying?" is the equivalent of, "What do you call home?" Jesus responds with an invitation to us all, "Come and see." Follow me, listen to my words, live as I live, do as I do. And you, too, shall be welcome where I stay.

Andrew played a supporting role in one of Jesus' miracles of the loaves and fishes. He was also present to witness one of Christ's most prophetic moments, when the Lord hinted at his own death and resurrection: *Now among those who went up to worship at the festival (Passover) were some Greeks. They came to Philip, who was from Bethsaida in Galilee, and said to him, "Sir, we wish to see Jesus." Philip went and told Andrew; then Andrew and Philip went and told Jesus. Jesus answered them. "The hour has come for the Son of Man to be glorified. Very truly, I tell you, unless a grain of wheat falls into the earth and dies, it remains just a single grain; but if it dies, it bears much fruit* (John 12:20-24).

In his Gospel, Mark mentions Andrew as being among a select few to whom Jesus spoke about the wars, earthquakes and famines of the last days, but also of hope associated with the Lord's second coming:

> *When he was sitting on the Mount of Olives opposite the temple, Peter, James, John and Andrew asked him privately, "Tell us, when will this be, and what will be the sign that all these things are about to be accomplished?" Then Jesus began to say to them....*
>
> *"But in those days, after that suffering, the sun will be darkened, and the moon will not give off its light, and the stars will be falling from the heavens, and the powers in the heavens will be shaken.*
>
> *Then they will see 'the Son of Man coming in the clouds' with great power and glory. Then he will send out the angels, and gather his elect from the four winds, from the ends of the earth to the ends of heaven* (Mark 13:3-4, 24-27).

Thinking back to the eleventh hole at Saint Andrews, one can conclude that Saint Andrews and the Bible have a great deal in common: While both provide challenges, ultimately the great course and the Good Book prove quite rewarding.

Saint Andrew isn't the only saint to influence a golf course. Saint Louis, patriarch of the city on the Mississippi as well as the Cardinal baseball team, lends his name to a country club in Clayton, Missouri.

Saint Louis, the course, is known for its par 3, 203-yard third hole, notable for its difficult putting surface, with its sharp front to back slope. Just to get to the dance floor one has to clear a pond while avoiding a number of bunkers surrounding the green, the most severe of which is a five-foot scoundrel cut into the ridge on which the green sits. Balls hit here are like Las Vegas—what lands in this bunker stays in this bunker. Saint Louis, the man, ascended the French throne at the age of thirteen under his mother's regency. He became King Louis IX at age twenty-one. Known for protecting the clergy from secular leaders, he led the sixth and seventh crusades. Imprisoned during the sixth crusade, he died of dysentery during the seventh.[7]

Saint George is famous on two continents as a golf course. Near Toronto, the course by that name hosts the Canadian Open, while Royal Saint George in Kent, known for its links, is one of the courses in the British Open Championship rotation. Long pictured as slaying the dragon and rescuing a fair maiden, Saint George the man was a favorite solider of Emperor Diocletian in the Roman army. However, during the emperor's persecution and murder of Christians during the third century, he tortured George before eventually beheading him. Because George steadfastly refused to renounce his faith, he is considered victorious over Satan. Thus, in the many heroic paintings of Saint George, the dragon represents wickedness and the maiden God's holy truth.[8]

Welsh Saint Enodoc lends his name to the course in Cornwall, England. Horribly abused by her stepmother as a child, Saint Germaine[9] has found serenity on the course bearing her name on the outskirts of Paris. Another French course—Saint Nom La Bretèche—takes its name from Saint Nonne, a bishop who helped re-evangelize the area after the Norman invasion.[10]

The San Francisco Golf Club, named after the city named after Saint Francis, boasts of its A.W. Tillinghast-inspired course. One of its holes—the par 3, 190-yard seventh—is named "The Duel," for the last known such event in America.[11] On the opposite end of the spectrum from arguments and weaponry is Saint Francis himself. Francis of Assisi, though born of a wealthy family, took a vow of poverty at age twenty. In the early 1200s he established the Franciscan Order, still in existence today. As a sign of his devotion to God, Francis was gifted with the stigmata: He physically retained on his hands and feet the wounds of Christ on the cross.[12] One of the most simple, yet hopeful prayers in all of Christianity is attributed to Francis. Appropriately titled the Prayer of Saint Francis,[13] it reads:

> *Lord, make me an instrument of your peace.*
> *where there is hatred, let me sow love;*
> *where there is injury, pardon;*
> *where there is doubt, faith;*
> *where there is despair, hope;*
> *where there is darkness, light;*
> *and where there is sadness, joy.*
> *O, Divine Master,*
> *grant that I may not so much seek*
> *to be consoled as to console;*
> *to be understood as to understand;*
> *to be loved as to love;*
> *for it is in giving that we receive;*
> *it is in pardoning that we are pardoned;*
> *and it is in dying that we are born to eternal life.*

While one of the criteria for canonization into sainthood is the attribution of miracles, there is no truth to the rumor, all evidence presented to the contrary, that candidates need to have a golf course named after them. But it can't hurt!

Too often we think of saints as being extremely holy, devoted, pious men and women willing to die for their faith. And for a good many, this was indeed the case. But there were those who showed very real signs of humanity, too. Saint Peter was headstrong and denied Jesus three times. Saint Thomas doubted that Christ rose from the dead. Saint Augustine had an illicit affair and fathered a son out of wedlock. Yet each overcame their flaws to live remarkable lives, serving God to the best of their ability, often inspiring great faith in others.

Saint George is famous on two continents as a golf course.

Sometimes we forget that saints are also people. By their examples, they show us what we are capable of accomplishing in the name of God. In the Apostles' Creed, we profess faith in "the communion of saints," the body of all souls destined for paradise. We are all born in the image and likeness of God. Christ died for our sins and showed us the way home to the Father. All of which is another way of saying that, just as we are all sinners, we all also have the capacity to be saints. It's like acknowledging that we are all duffers but could also shoot par if we just stayed on the straight and narrow fairway of life.

# Augusta and Apostles

One of the charter members of what is now the United States Golfing Association is the Chicago Golf Club[1] located in Wheaton, Illinois. Founded in 1894, it is the country's oldest 18-hole course. Among these 18 ancients is one hole in particular that tests a golfer's mettle as well as elicits praise for its design: the 440-yard, par 4 twelfth, more commonly known as The Punch Bowl.[2]

A blind tee shot over a slight hill must elude five bunkers scattered from tee to elevated green. Guarding the entrance to the putting area is a deep-faced bunker on the front right. Giving the hole its name is the fact that the green rises on all sides, funneling the ball to the middle of the green, which is fine, if that's where the flagstick is. The verdant surface itself is full of humps and bumps inviting golfers to take their lumps.

Another great twelfth was the site of a thirteenth. Tiger Woods' 2007 PGA Championship win at Southern Hills in Tulsa, Oklahoma, gave him his thirteenth major title. Woods once again displayed his virtuosity, using any number of numbered clubs in his bag to drive from the different tees: a two-iron, three-iron, four-iron, five-iron, three-wood and driver. He joins an eclectic but noteworthy group who have won majors at the Tulsa course: U. S. Open winners Tommy Bolt (1958), Hubert Green (1977) and Retief Goosen (2001), and PGA champions Dave Stockton (1970), Raymond Floyd (1982) and Nick Price (1994).

More gentle than steep, Southern Hills still provides a stern test for those who play there, especially in the dogleg days of August. That no one player has dominated the course speaks volumes as to its difficult but fair play. Representative of the varied challenges on the course is the 445-yard, par 4 twelfth hole. A couple of guys who knew a swing or two about golf, Arnold Palmer and Ben Hogan, thought quite highly of this hole. Hogan went so far as to exclaim that the twelfth at Southern Hills was "the greatest par four in the United States."[3]

A slight dogleg left, with a large sand trap at the elbow, the hole calls for a blind drive off the tee to a landing area that takes advantage of the right to left slope of the fairway. Should one be skillful enough to avoid the oak and elm trees and full rough, there's another blind shot to be taken. This mid iron's charge is to carry a water hazard near the front of the elevated green while avoiding the meandering, yet menacing, water on the right side of the approach. A too rambunctious effort may find one of three large oval bunkers to the left and behind the green. Sloped from back to front, the quick, slick-putting surface presents its own problems. All in all, the combination brings a new meaning to the term "Southern" hospitality.

To everyone from the touring pro to the weekend duffer to those who know nothing about golf, one tournament stands tall in all the land: The Masters. In 1934, none other than Bobby Jones, an early master of the game, along with Clifford Roberts, originated the tournament to be played by only the best golfers in the nation.[4] Initially called the Augusta National Invitational, it became known as the Masters five years later. Played over the first Thursday through Sunday in April at the beautiful Augusta National Golf Club in Augusta, Georgia, the Masters is the only one of the four grand slam events to be played every year at the same venue. A fairway-green colored blazer may not make any GQ list of essentials for the modern man, but such a jacket, when adorned with the Augusta National Golf Club logo (first presented to Sam Snead in 1949), is the envy of golfers everywhere. A look at multiple winners showcases some of the most famous names in the sport:

| | |
|---|---|
| 6 times: | Jack Nicklaus—1963, 1965, 1966, 1972, 1975, 1986 |
| 4 times: | Arnold Palmer—1958, 1960, 1962, 1964 |
| | Tiger Woods—1997, 2001, 2002, 2005 |
| 3 times: | Jimmy DeMaret—1940, 1947, 1950 |
| | Sam Snead—1949, 1952, 1954 |
| | Gary Player—1961, 1974, 1978 |
| | Nick Faldo—1989, 1990, 1996 |
| 2 times: | Horton Smith—1934, 1936 |
| | Byron Nelson—1937, 1942 |
| | Ben Hogan—1951, 1953 |
| | Tom Watson—1977, 1981 |
| | Seve Ballesteros—1980, 1983 |
| | Bernhard Langer—1985, 1993 |
| | Ben Crenshaw—1984, 1995 |
| | Jose Maria Olazabal—1994, 1999 |
| | Phil Mickelson—2004, 2006 |

Bobby Jones and course architect Alister MacKenzie, he of Cypress Point renown, joined forces to design Augusta National. The names of the individual holes conjure up a stroll in a picturesque garden: Pink Dogwood, Magnolia, Juniper, Yellow Jasmine, Carolina Cherry, Camellia, White Dogwood, Azalea, Redbud.[5] A look at how the course plays, however, recalls Mark Twain's much-repeated quote: "Golf is a good walk spoiled."

Take the twelfth hole for instance. A short par 3 at 155 yards, this test of courage is named Golden Bell after a bright yellow flowering shrub in the olive family. To play the Golden Bell correctly, take the advice of the Golden Bear: Aim for just over the front bunker and shade to the side on which the hole is placed.[6] Otherwise, an iron shot off the green must deal with Rae's Creek and one bunker in front of the green and two bunkers and a stand of stately pines at the rear. Depending upon the swirling winds, anywhere from a six- to nine-iron is the club of choice off the tee. In 1988 Curtis Strange aced this hole.[7] Others have been far less fortunate. For instance, eight years earlier Tom Weiskopf accumulated a thirteen.[8]

In the New Testament, the number twelve is significant as that is the number chosen by Christ to be his apostles. Think of these select as three very fortunate foursomes. (Of course, one of the original players disqualified himself, but he was replaced quickly by another who was eager to play.)

Matthew is a good example of how Jesus chose those he recruited. A little background: Tax collectors were usually Jews working for the Roman government. Any money they collected over and above what was owed Rome would inevitably line their pockets. Needless to say, they were not well liked among their brethren, as their wealth came at the people's expense. Thus, when most everyone else Matthew came in contact with wanted very little to do with him, Jesus chose this tax collector to be included in his inner circle. As for some of the other apostles, turn to Luke: *Once while Jesus was standing beside the lake of Gennesaret, and the crowd was pressing in on him to hear the word of God, he saw two boats there at the shore of the lake; the fishermen had gone out of them and were washing their nets. He got into one of the boats, the one belonging to Simon, and asked him to put out a little way from the shore. Then he sat down and taught the crowds from the boat. When he had finished speaking, he said to Simon, 'Put out into the deep water and let down your nets for a catch.' Simon answered, 'Master, we have worked all night long but have caught nothing. Yet if you say so, I will let down the nets.' When they had done this, they caught so many fish that their nets were beginning to break. So they signaled to their partners in the other boat to come and help them. And they came and filled both boats, so that they began to sink. But when Simon Peter saw it, he fell down at Jesus' knees, saying, 'Go away from me, Lord, for I am a sinful man!' For he and all who were with him were amazed at the catch of fish that they had taken; and so also were James and John, sons of Zebedee, who were partners with Simon. Then Jesus said to Simon, 'Do not be afraid; from now on you will be catching people.' When they had brought their boats to shore, they left everything and followed him* (Luke 5:1-11).

In John's Gospel, we learn of others "joining the golf outing": *The next day Jesus decided to go to Galilee. He found Philip and said to him, 'Follow me.' Now Philip was from Bethsaida, the city of Andrew and Peter. Philip found Nathanael and said to him, 'We have found him about whom Moses in the law and also the prophets wrote, Jesus son of Joseph from Nazareth.' Nathanael said to him, 'Can anything good come out of Nazareth?' Philip said to him, 'Come and see.' When Jesus saw Nathanael coming towards him, he said of him, 'Here is truly an Israelite in whom there is no deceit!' Nathanael asked him, 'Where did you come to know me?' Jesus answered, 'I saw you under the fig tree before Philip called you.' Nathanael* replied, *'Rabbi, you are the Son of God! You are the King of Israel!' Jesus answered, 'Do you believe because I told you that I saw you under the fig tree? You will see greater things than these.' And he said to him, 'Very truly, I tell you, you will see heaven opened and the angels of God ascending and descending upon the Son of Man '*(John 1:43-51).

Though Nazareth is well known today as the place where Jesus was raised, during the period he called it home, it was a tiny village of no importance. Thus Nathanael's statement, *"Can anything good come out of Nazareth?"* Jesus' hometown was so small, so insignificant that one truly had to wonder if anything worthwhile could come from such a place, especially someone important.

One can imagine similar thoughts going through golfers' and fans' minds when newcomers arrive on the PGA scene. Can this son of a gold miner be any good? Can this former member of the Coast Guard take the pressure of the tour? Can this guy who taught himself how to play with hand-me-down clubs win a major? Well, for golf Hall of Famers Gary Player, Arnold Palmer and Lee Trevino, respectively, the answer was obviously, "Darn straight!"

As for the complete list of apostolic foursomes, Luke and Mark summarize it this way: *Now during those days he went out to the mountain to pray; and he spent the night in prayer to God. And when the day came, he called his disciples and chose twelve of them, whom he also named apostles: Simon (to whom he gave the name Peter) and his brother Andrew.... James son of Zebedee and John the brother of James (to whom he gave the name Boanerges, that is Sons of Thunder)...and Philip, Bartholomew (Nathanael), and Matthew, and Thomas, and James son of Alphaeus, and Thaddaeus, and Simon the Cananaean, and Judas Iscariot, who betrayed him* (Luke 6:12-14; Mark 3:17-19).

🏌 🏌 🏌

That Jesus prayed and sought his Father's counsel before deciding upon his apostles should come as no surprise. As the Son of God, Jesus always turned to prayer to discern his Father's wishes. Christ would often use prayer to refocus his energies on his mission, to reconnect with his Father, our God. These times must have been very tender moments between Father and Son, just as our prayers with God can be like intimate conversations between a parent and an adult child.

And if the gospels are any indication, there were instances when the Lord felt abandoned and alone, in need of consolation and fortitude: *And after he had dismissed the crowds, he went up to the mountains by himself to pray* (Matthew 14:23).

Though divine, Jesus was also very much human. Inevitably, he would have needed to get away if only for a moment's peace of mind, so that he could do his work again another day. Jesus often repaired to the wilderness. How often have we found a walk in the woods, a stroll along an ocean beach, a mountain hike, fly-fishing along a scenic river to be revitalizing? God created the skies and the trees and the green grass of the earth. So it's no wonder that God can always be found on a golf course, if you look.

Prayer can be described as a quieting of the mind, a refocusing of our hearts on God's purpose for us. Prayer is conversation with our Father. One way to think of our purpose on earth is to be in right relationship with our Creator. As with any relationship, bonds are formed through conversations. And as with any form of conversation, prayer is equal parts speaking and listening. For most of us, it's easy to do the talking. We ask God for help, forgiveness, understanding, consolation. There may come times when we pray for guidance, whether it be in choosing the right career, wondering if a certain someone is our true soul mate, or even what club to use for our approach shot to an uphill green. We give thanks for our children, a sunset, a recovery, breaking par. And God answers our prayer: *"Ask, and it will be given to you; search, and you will find; knock, and the door will be opened*

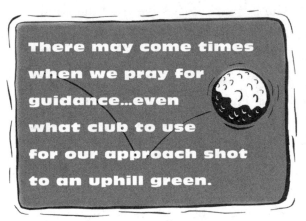

> **There may come times when we pray for guidance...even what club to use for our approach shot to an uphill green.**

*to you. For everyone who asks receives, and everyone who searches finds, and for everyone who knocks, the door will be opened. Is there anyone among you who, if your child asks for bread, will give a stone? Or if the child asks for a fish, will he give a snake? If you then, who are evil, know how to give good gifts to your children, how much more will your Father in heaven give good things to those who ask him!"* (Matthew 7:7-11).

As for how we should lead our lives, Jesus taught that as well:

> *"Therefore do not worry, saying, 'What will we eat?' or 'What will we drink?' or 'What will we wear?' For it is the Gentiles who strive for all these things; and indeed your heavenly Father knows that you need all these things. But strive first for the kingdom of God and his righteousness, and all these things will be given to you as well.*
>
> *"So do not worry about tomorrow, for tomorrow will bring worries of its own. Today's trouble is enough for today"* (Matthew 6:31-34).

*"But I say to you that listen: Love your enemies, do good*
*to those who hate you, bless those who curse you, pray for those*
*who abuse you...Give to everyone who begs from you...Do to*
*others as you would have them do to you...Be merciful, just as*
*your Father is merciful"* (Luke 6:27-28, 30-31, 36).

Consider those Jesus chose to be his disciples, his handpicked followers upon whom the fate of the fledgling church would rest. Peter admitted he was a sinful man. Matthew was scorned as a pawn of the Roman government. James and John argued about who would sit at God's right hand. Nathanael was initially skeptical about Jesus and his ministry. Later in the gospels, we learn that Thomas was a cynic, thus the term "doubting Thomas." Mary Magdalene was possessed by evil spirits.

Jesus did not choose the righteous, the powerful, the influential, the rich. He chose the sinner, skeptic, cynic, possessed. In other words, Christ has chosen us. Through his teachings, preaching, passion, death and resurrection, the Son of God has redeemed us all.

Think about this for a second. The group that Jesus assembled to bring God's word to the world consisted of four fishermen, a tax collector, possibly a farmer or two, maybe a baker, and a handful of women. Chances are Jesus himself learned the trade of a carpenter. If after pondering the incredibleness of it all, you still have trouble believing that you have a role in all of this, then think about this for a second: Golf, a sport played all over the world by millions and at a very skilled level by a few, first started out as a simple game where a ball was hit into a hole in the ground with a hickory stick. If golf can come as far as it has, so can we become the disciples that Jesus sought and needs.

# The Amen Corner

In this, the thirteenth hole of the book, we make a return visit to three courses already mentioned. At Oak Hill, golfers on the thirteenth hole face a stern test on a nearly 600-yard par 5. Not only does the hole play uphill, there's a slight dogleg to the right, requiring three shots to make the green. Long drivers must also pause and consider Allen's Creek, which crosses the fairway at the halfway point. Ideally, a wood shot would avoid bunkers along the right of the fairway while at the same time lining up the subsequent iron. This third stroke needs to soar high in order to overcome the steep hill area before the green. Once on the putting surface, you have to deal with a bowl-like contour that slopes sharply from back to front. As if all this were not enough, the green in ringed by bunkers, two at the front, a half dozen behind.

When is a 448-yard par 4 not a par 4? When it's the thirteenth hole at Pine Valley. From an upper or lower tee, a drive must carry across an expanse of what can best be described as New Jersey prairie to an uphill, crowned fairway. And this is quite possibly the easiest shot of the hole. From there, the safe golfer (read: weak of heart) will play across a narrow valley area to a second fairway to the right of the green. Such a shot would need to carry the crest of fairway two to leave a manageable iron to the green. The confident golfer (read: at times foolhardy) will choose to launch a behemoth second shot across an area of pine trees, scrub brush, sand, and steep walls in the hope of finding the green. It's not surprising that many a ball is lost in this tangle. What is surprising is that some golfers are not lost trying to find said balls. Once on the green, the benumbed amateur (or even pro) finds the uneven surface presents its own set of problems. Only those whose ability matches their fearlessness have a chance to reach the green in two, and thus a chance at par. Most others consider the hole vanquished with a bogey. (Still others are happy with enough balls left in their bag to continue playing the rest of this diabolical course.)

As for a combination of beauty and danger, take a tour of the thirteenth at Augusta. Georgia pines, Rae's creek, multi-colored azaleas in full bloom, bright greens and white sand bunkers supply the scenery. A near 90-degree dogleg, woods left and right, said creek and bunkers, and a steep slope around the green provide the menace.

As a matter of fact, golfing lore has lent a bit of the divine to the Azalea Hole, for holes eleven, twelve and thirteen at Augusta constitute the Amen Corner. According to the FAQs at www.masters. org the term "was first coined in a 1958 *Sports Illustrated* article by Herbert Warren Wind, who…was searching for an appropriate name for the location where the critical action had taken place that year. He borrowed the name from an old jazz recording *Shouting at Amen Corner* by a band under the direction of Milton (Mezz) Mezzrow, a Chicago clarinetist."[1]

As to the tournament in question, John Boyette of *The Augusta Chronicle* recalled this play. On Saturday evening heavy rains soaked the course. For Sunday's round, a local rule was adopted allowing a player whose ball was embedded to lift and drop it without penalty. Sunday on hole twelve, Arnold Palmer hit his ball over the green and the ball embedded in the steep bank behind it. Being uncertain about the applicability of the local rule, the official on the hole and Palmer agreed that the ball should be played as it lay and that Palmer could play a second ball, which he dropped. Palmer holed out for a five with the original ball and a three with the second ball. The committee was asked to decide if the local rule was applicable in this case and, if so, which of Arnie's scores should count. At thirteen, still unsure of what his score was on twelve, Palmer sank an 18-foot putt for eagle three. When he was playing fifteen, Palmer was told his drop on twelve was proper and that his score on the hole was three, leading to his first major victory.[2] Amen, indeed!

"Amen" is Bible-speak for "so be it." Most people recognize the term as the concluding remark commonly used in prayers. How fitting that three consecutive holes at Augusta should be called Amen Corner. After all, how many players have uttered silent prayers of thanks for having negotiated the trio successfully?

How many players have uttered silent prayers of thanks for having negotiated the trio at Augusta successfully?

Amen also plays a declarative role in the Bible. One of the first times the word appears is in Psalm 106 in the Old Testament. In this poem, meant to be sung as a hymn, the psalmist opens with a verse of praise, then a lengthy apology for the sins of Israel, concluding with prayers of hope:

> *Praise the Lord!*
> *O give thanks to the Lord, for he is good;*

*for his steadfast love endures for ever.*
*...Many times he delivered them* (the Jews),
*but they were rebellious in their purposes,*
*and were brought low through their iniquity.*
*Nevertheless, he* (God) *regarded their distress*
     *when he heard their cry.*
*For their sake he remembered his covenant,*
*and showed compassion,*
          *according to the abundance of his steadfast love.*
*He caused them to be pitied by all who held them captive.*
*Save us, O Lord our God,*
          *and gather us from among the nations,*
*that we may give thanks to your holy name*
          *and glory in your praise.*
*Blessed be the Lord, the God of Israel,*
*from everlasting to everlasting.*
*And let all the people say, "Amen."*
*Praise the Lord!* (Psalm 106: 1, 43-48).

Though not noted in more modern translations, biblical footnotes inform us that ancient authorities concluded each of the gospels with "Amen." With each amen comes a concluding ring of authority:

*Now the eleven disciples went to Galilee, to the mountain*
*to which Jesus had directed them. When they saw him, they*
*worshiped him; but some doubted. And Jesus came and said to*
*them, "All authority in heaven and on earth had been given to*
*me. Go therefore and make disciples of all nations, baptizing them*
*in the name of the Father and of the Son and of the Holy Spirit,*

*and teaching them to obey everything that I have commanded you. And remember, I am with you always, to the end of the age. Amen" (Matthew 28:16-20).*

*So then the Lord Jesus, after he had spoken to them, was taken up into heaven and sat down at the right hand of God. And they went out and proclaimed the good news everywhere, while the Lord worked with them and confirmed the message by the signs that accompanied it. Amen (Mark 16:19-20).*

*Then he said to them, "These are my words that I spoke to you while I was still with you—that everything written about me in the law of Moses, the prophets, and the psalms must be fulfilled." Then he opened their minds to understand the scriptures, and he said to them, "Thus it is written, that the Messiah is to suffer and to rise from the dead on the third day, and that repentance and forgiveness of sins is to be proclaimed in his name to all nations, beginning from Jerusalem. You are witnesses of these things. And see, I am sending upon you what my Father promised; so stay here in the city until you have been clothed with power from on high."*

*Then he led them out as far as Bethany, and lifting his hands, he blessed them. While he was blessing them, he withdrew from them and was carried up into heaven. And they worshipped him, and returned to Jerusalem with great joy; and they were continually in the temple blessing God. Amen (Luke 24:44-53).*

*This is the disciple who is testifying to these things and has written them, and we know that his testimony is true. But there are also many other things that Jesus did; if every one of them were*

*written down, I suppose that the world itself could not contain*
*that books that would be written. Amen (John 21:24-25).*

So be it that all that has been written is true. So be it that God
said, "Tee it up."

To which we say, "Amen to that!"

# Clubs and Talents

Having played at the finest courses all over the world, many golfers have a great appreciation for the art and architecture that go into the design of 18 unique holes. Some of the most recognized players the game has known have turned their attention to the building of courses that reflect their personalities and love of the game. Bobby Jones helped design Augusta National; Arnold Palmer, Bay Hill; Gary Player, the eponymous Gary Player Country Club in Sun City, South Africa; Tom Watson, the Links at Spanish Bay in Pebble Beach; Tom Weiskopf, the Loch Lomond Golf Club in Scotland.

However, none have left their combined mark of championship play and championship courses as strongly as Jack Nicklaus. In addition to his eighteen major championships, the Golden Bear can lay claim to a number of world-class golf courses. Through his firm, Nicklaus Design, that number happens to be more than 300, including 84 that have hosted more than 588 professional tournaments.[1] Among Nicklaus' notable designs are Harbor Town in Hilton Head and Muirfield Village in Dublin, Ohio, home of the Memorial Tournament.

Golf is every bit as much a mental game as it is physical. Not only must players contend with the performance of the competition, they must also duel with their own doubt and desire. One hole at Muirfield—the fourteenth—offers players many opportunities to do just that. At 363 yards, this par 4 might suggest a birdie opportunity to many. With a downhill tee shot to a wide, tree-lined fairway, the hole opens with promise. It's at this point, however, when contemplating the approach, that your mind may play havoc with your game. Just the slightest doubt in club or shot selection can disrupt what should be a fairly straightforward approach. No doubt the meandering creek that wraps itself around the right hand side of the green tempts players to shade left. Or perhaps it's the large sand trap on the left that moves ball strikers to hit right. Then again, because the green is so long and narrow, there isn't much margin for error left or right. All of which means that before one even gets to the "dance floor," the pressure is on for a near perfect shot. At this point, those earlier thoughts of a birdie tend to fly away, like a—well—little birdie.

Shinnecock Hills in Southhampton, New York, offers another killer fourteenth. As if playing the lay of the land and eluding the hazards a golf course presents aren't challenge enough, often Mother Nature allows a swirling breeze or two to further confound golfers. Most courses have holes that run parallel to one another, the tee of one near the green of another. In layouts such as this, at least a golfer can adapt to the wind fairly easily. It will be blowing in one of two ways. Except at Shinnecock Hills. To take advantage of the ocean breezes, architects William Davis, William Flynn and Howard Toomey configured a majority of the holes to run in different directions from one another. With so many bends in the course, golfers need constantly need to figure out how the wind will affect each shot. In fact, the second and third and the eleventh and twelfth are the only consecutive holes that run in the same direction.[2] Add to this challenge the natural rolling hills and valleys, sandy scrub and sea grasses of the course, and no wonder Shinnecock is praised (or sometimes damned?) for its test of skill.

At the fourteenth, for instance, golfers begin at an elevated tee where a drive must clear scrub to an undulating fairway that eases right. Bordered on the left by bunkers and right by steep rough, the fairway narrows to an open green that invites low running shots. Make that *well-placed* low running shots as large bunkers, two left and one right short of the green, are poised to gobble up wayward balls. Make that *well-placed* and *well-paced* low running shots as the green, sitting in a saddle atop a slope, falls off on the backside. Club and shot selection will vary from day to day, even hour to hour, as winds may change direction or velocity at a moment's notice.

While Muirfield Village presents challenges in the form of clever design, and Shinnecock Hills allows nature to provide the test, there are some courses or holes that do away with subtlety and offer bold, brash, brazen, even diabolical elements to be navigated about. One such hole is number fourteen at Saint Andrews Old. A shade over 400 yards from the tee yet still some 170 yards from the pin resides a bunker so deep, so cavernous that its very name instills fear in the most-skilled players on the planet. Some bunkers are constructed by bulldozer; this one could have been made by a meteorite. A ten-foot-deep crater, it goes by the name of Hell Bunker.[3] One reason for it being so called may be that once you go in, you may never get out. In the 1995 British Open, none other than Jack Nicklaus had the unfortunate experience of placing his second shot in Hell. It took him four strokes to escape, helping to boost his tally for the hole to an un-Golden-Bearable ten.[4] What hope then is there for us mere mortals?

Thus far, the "literary links" in this book have covered fourteen holes, incorporating bunkers as big as craters, sand traps reminiscent of African deserts, blind tee shots, Alps, punch bowls, postage stamps, scrub brush, tall grass, gorse, trains, trees, trenches, quarries, bowls, burns, rivers, ponds, lakes, ocean inlets, rough, fringe, out of bounds, undulating greens, sloping surfaces, church pews, chasms, up hills, down hills, headwinds, tail winds, cross winds, pinched fairways and upside down saucers.

Whew!

With so many conditions to play, not to mention distances to cover, how does one choose the right club? That's where the number fourteen comes to play. Fortunately, golfing rules state a player may select up to fourteen clubs with which to play a round of golf. As to which clubs to choose, that depends on a player's ability and the conditions or difficulty of the course. Ben Hogan, for example did not carry a 7-iron during the 1950 U.S. Open at Merion County Club in Ohio because, he said, "There are no 7-iron shots at Merion."[5] For which clubs to carry, golf.about.com suggests the following arrays.[6]

For the high-handicap golfer, that is the person who is as likely to hit a car with his or her own drive as the fairway: 3-wood, 5-wood, 7-wood; 5-iron through 9-iron; pitching wedge; putter. Though not fourteen clubs, this assortment is adequate for most weekend golfers. Any more weapons in the bag and the high-handicapper is courting more disaster than usual. The small forest, that is the three woods, are needed because beginning golfers have little or no control whatsoever over a driver. Consider the woods to be Big Bertha's little brothers. One could argue that given the amount of time beginners spend in sand traps that a sand wedge would be in order. However, given the novice's lack of finesse with wedges (and I should know) the pitching version falls into the one-wedge-fits-all category.

The mid-handicap golfer is the person who can actually make par enough times per round to suggest a false sense of progress. Such players will then often invest heavily in just about any kind of golfing equipment imaginable to give them extra length on their drives, control of their irons and a soft touch on the greens. Thirteen clubs are listed here, giving the mid-capper the option for another iron or wedge depending upon the requirements of the course: driver; 3-wood, 5-wood, 7-wood; 4-iron through 9-iron; pitching wedge; sand wedge; putter.

For the low handicap golfer, that is someone who has more pars than bogeys and is skillful enough to make competent shots look like good fortune in order to fleece playing partners of friendly wagers, the club assortment may be like the following: driver; 3-wood; 2-iron through 9-iron; pitching wedge; lob wedge; sand wedge; putter. Low handicappers have

Jack Nicklaus had the unfortunate experience of placing his second shot in Hell.

much better control of their driver and 3-wood so they are able to trade the remaining woods for lower irons. Adding a lob wedge gives the player more options in and around the green.

Just as golf gives players the tools with which to play the game, God provides people with gifts or talents with which to experience life. He expects us to nurture them and share them to the best of our abilities: *"For it is as if a man, going on a journey, summoned his slaves and entrusted his property to them; to one he gave five talents, to another two, to another one, to each according to his ability. Then he went away.*

The one who had received the five talents went off at once and traded with them, and made five more talents. In the same way, the one who had the two talents made two more talents. But the one who received one talent went off and dug a hole in the ground and hid his master's money. After a long time the master of those slaves came and settled accounts with them. Then the one who had received five talents came forward, bringing five more talents, saying, 'Master, you handed over to me five talents; see, I have made five more talents.' His master said to him, 'Well done, good and trustworthy slave; you have been trustworthy in a few things, I will put you in charge of many things; enter into the joy of your master.' And the one with the two talents also came forward, saying, "Master, you handed over to me two talents; see, I have made two more talents.' His master said to him, 'Well done, good and trustworthy slave; you have been trustworthy in a few things, I will put you in charge of many things; enter into the joy of your master.' Then the one who had received one talent also came forward, saying, 'Master, I knew that you were a harsh man, reaping where you did not sow, and gathering where you did not scatter seed; so I was afraid, and I went and hid your talent in the ground. Here you have what is yours.' But his master replied, 'You wicked and lazy slave! You knew, did you, that I reap where I do not sow, and gather where I did not scatter? Then you ought to have invested my money with the bankers, and on my return I would have received what was my own with interest. So take the talent from him, and give it to the one with the ten talents. For to all those who have, more will be given, and they will have an abundance; but from those who have nothing, even what they have will be taken away. As for this worthless slave, throw him into the outer darkness, where there will be weeping and gnashing of teeth" (Matthew 25:14-30).

On the links, as in life, there have been individuals who have been given unique gifts that have allowed them to flourish. And there have been those who have been given talents and squandered them.

Ben Hogan, for example, worked tirelessly on his form to own what many have called the best swing in the game. Phil Mickelson is known for his deft left touch with a wedge; John Daly for his prodigious drives. On his way to winning eighteen major tournaments, Jack Nicklaus earned a well-deserved reputation for exceptional putting. Tiger Woods is acclaimed for his complete game, having virtually mastered every conceivable shot needed on a golf course. Tiger indeed has nurtured five talents: the ability to drive straight and true, skill with any number of irons, accurate putting even from great distances, incredible recovery shots and strategic course management.

Despite his reputation as being one of the longest hitters in the game, on the other hand, John Daly is thought by some to have squandered his talents. Long John burst upon the PGA scene during the 1991 PGA Championship. When Nick Price was forced to drop out, Daly became the ninth, and final, alternate offered a spot in the field. Having no practice round, Daly posted an opening tally of sixty-nine. Three other solid rounds and the former Arkansas Razorback won his first major in zero-to-hero fashion. In 1995, he repeated the scenario with an unexpected victory in the British Open at Saint Andrews, defeating Italian Costantino Rocca in a playoff.[7]

Overweight, smoking and cola-drinking non-stop, and sporting a mullet, Daly had become a fan favorite of the everyman. However, bouts with heavy drinking derailed his career. He has entered alcohol addiction programs on more than one occasion. It's estimated that he lost in the neighborhood of $50-$60 million dollars in gambling. This lifestyle took its toll, resulting in three divorces.[8] He went more than five years without winning a tournament.

As the gospel of Matthew relates, talent not nurtured is talent buried: *"For to all those who have, more will be given, and they will have an abundance; but from those who have nothing, even what they have will be taken away"* (Matthew 25: 29).

We are all given certain gifts from our Creator. We may not be able to drive a golf ball 300 yards or chip to within four feet of the cup. But some of us have the ability to speak foreign languages or play the flute. Others are able to write software code or discover cures for diseases. Still others can walk on I-beams or mine for coal. Regardless of the nature of our gifts or the quantity, we all have the capacity to love—the game of golf and one another.

# The Sistine Chapel of Golf

Every year one Jack Nicklaus-designed course—the Desert Mountain Golf Club—hosts the Senior PGA Tradition event. Set in the sunny climes of Scottsdale, Arizona, the Cochise course features a rather unique green at the fifteenth. A near 550-yard par 5 offers players a slim to slimmer chance to reach the green in two. Slim to slimmer because the green, when looked at from above, resembles a classic soft drink bottle in shape. Most players take two shots to set up a manageable iron from a safe distance. Still, even that shot has little margin for error, as the green is virtually surrounded by water on all sides. That little margin for error is even less when the rock hazards are taken into account. A player hitting a ball into these piles runs the risk of it bouncing all the way to New Mexico or embedding itself in a nook or cranny. Playing it from there is a good way to snap a club in two. By way of analogy, if the golf ball represented the earth, the size of these stones would resemble Jupiter. Houston, we have a problem.

Even when a hole is free of hazards, traps, bunkers, scrub, tall trees in the middle of the fairway, meandering creeks, roads or nearby railways, a test of skill awaits. Such is the case at hole fifteen at Pine Valley. Fairly tame by Pine Valley standards, the 600-plus yard par 5 is l-o-n-g. Once a lake is carried, the fairway runs unobstructed toward the uphill green. Simple enough, right? However, the closer you get to the green, the more exact the shots must become. What had been a 60-yard expanse of fairway is now a mere twenty paces across at the putting surface. Moreover, pine trees constantly encroach upon the fairway until the green seems surrounded by them.

Of all the courses in the world—Saint Andrews with its treachery and traditions, Pine Valley with its severity and variety, Augusta with flowers in bloom and jackets of green, Sand Hills with its natural beauty, and countless others—an argument can be made that the most notable, beautiful and challenging of them all is the Cypress Point Club at Pebble Beach. It has been called the Sistine Chapel of Golf.[1] And no wonder. Every hole is a work of art.

Course architect Alister MacKenzie had the help of a creative mastermind with the design of Cypress Point. That collaborator of course was Almighty God, the Ultimate Creator. MacKenzie took all that God provided and adapted it to a course unparalleled in grandeur and excitement. Perhaps the one hole that captures the spirit of Cypress Point is the fifteenth. At 139 yards, what this par 3 lacks in length it makes up for in stomach-churning angst. Separating tee and green is a chasm formed by a finger of the Pacific Ocean some sixty feet below that reaches in to touch the craggy coast. The green is surrounded by white sand traps. Surrounding the traps is a grove of cypress trees on the left and ice plant, rock face and ocean blue on the right. It takes a fearless iron off the tee to land close to the flagstick in order to make bird. Birdie or bogey, one comes away with an awe-inspired appreciation of the beauty of God's creation.

By virture of being compared to the Sistine Chapel, Cypress Point brings a definite connection between the Bible and the game of golf to the discussion. Completed in the 1480s, the Capella Sistina is named after Pope Sixtus IV who commissioned its construction. On August 9, 1483, the chapel was dedicated to the Virgin Mary on the Feast of the Assumption. Traditionally, it is used as the papal chapel for small masses and meetings. Most notably, it is the place where the

College of Cardinals meets as a conclave to elect a new pope.[2]

For most of the world, the Sistine Chapel is renowned for its beautiful frescoes and painted ceilings, seemingly in three dimensions, depicting stories from the Bible. Originally, the ceiling was painted a brilliant blue with gold stars. However, Pope Julius II asked Michelangelo to bring his artistry to the chapel. Between the years 1508 and 1512, the artist brought color and form to tales of the Old Testament.

From the Book of Genesis came visualizations of creation with God dividing light from darkness, creating the sun and the moon, and separating water from land. In perhaps one of the most famous and recognizable images in the world, the artist depicted the creation of man. God the Father reaches out with the touch of life, his finger having just graced that of Adam. Eve's creation is also illustrated, as is the original sin. Three scenes from the life of Noah are represented: the sacrifice of Noah, the deluge, and his drunkenness: *The Lord saw that the wickedness of humankind was great in the earth, and that every inclination of the thoughts was only evil continually. And the Lord was sorry that he made humankind on the earth, and it grieved him to his heart. So the Lord said, "I will blot out from the earth the human beings that I have created — people together with animals and creeping things and birds of the air, for I am sorry that I made them." But Noah found favor in the sight of the Lord* (Genesis 6:5-8).

Fast forward to God's covenant with Noah after the flood: *"I will never again curse the ground because of humankind, for the inclination of the human heart is evil from youth; nor will I ever again destroy every living creature as I have done. As long as the earth endures, seedtime and harvest, cold and heat, summer and winter, day and night shall not cease.... When the [rain]bow is in the clouds I will see it and remember the everlasting covenant between God and every living creature of all flesh that is on the earth." God said to Noah, "This is the sign of the covenant that I have established between me and all flesh that is on the earth"* (Genesis 8:21-22; 9:16-17).

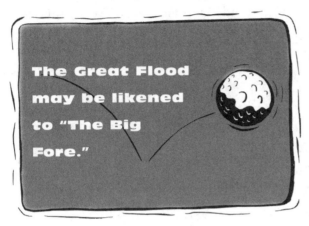

The Great Flood may be likened to "The Big Fore." To anyone who has ever hit a wayward shot on a golf course, "fore" is the exclamation of warning to those nearby that a white dimpled spherical missile may be coming toward them at great speed from unexpected directions. In Genesis, God is giving himself a mulligan, a do over, regarding the creation of humankind and the animal kingdom. After all, what God has given God can take easily away. There are several parallels between the first tale of creation with Adam and Eve and the second with Noah and his family. Given the human tendency to lust, to covet, for boastfulness and pride, to ignore the earth and each other, in general to sin, perhaps readers of the Bible need two stories to reinforce our sinful nature and God's willingness to forgive and allow us a fresh start.

Other scenes from the Old Testament that adorn the Sistine ceiling include the punishment of Hamon, Moses and the bronze serpent, David and Goliath, and Judith and Holofernes. Most people have heard of the story of David and Goliath—how a young boy handpicked by God to lead the Hebrews, slays the giant by means of a rock and sling, leading to the rout of the Philistines. David goes onto to become King of Israel, and from his line Jesus descends. However, not as many folks are as familiar with Judith, one of the heroines of the Bible, who played a similar role.

Somewhere in the neighborhood of 100 to 200 years before Christ, the Jews were about to be attacked by King Nebuchadnezzar's powerful Assyrian army, under the command of General Holofernes. A widow still in mourning, Judith took it upon herself to outwit and defeat the general in order to inspire the Jewish army to victory.

Losing her sackcloth and widow's demeanor, Judith dressed herself to showcase her very beautiful features and crossed over to the enemy camp ostensibly to reveal secrets about how to crush the Jewish forces. Understandably, the Assyrian general fell under her spell:

> *For she put away her widow's clothing*
> *to exalt the oppressed in Israel.*
> *She anointed her face with perfume;*
> *and fastened her hair with a tiara*
> *and put on a linen gown to beguile him.*
> *Her sandal ravished his eyes,*
> *her beauty captivated his mind.* (Judith 16:7-9)

Earning the general's confidence, Judith was invited to party with him one night. Hoping to bed her, the military man got, not to put too fine a point on it, dead drunk. Judith then took the general's sword...and beheaded him! She brought Holofernes' head back to her village of Bethulia to inspire the troops to overcome the Assyrian army, which became frightened with the loss of their commander.

Not many of us would be brave enough to enter the camp of our enemies armed with nothing more than our personal appearance to slay an oppressive leader. However, earlier in the Book of Judith she offers some words that we would do well to heed even in these modern times.

Being human, we often look to take the easier path. We seek to shirk undesirable duties. We make deals with the Almighty. It may be a response to serious wake up call: Dear God, I promise to give up smoking if you allow me to beat my lung cancer. It may be something less drastic: Dear Lord, if you help me pass my chemistry final I'll go to church regularly. It may even be a trifle: Hey, God, if you let me make this tricky putt, I will donate my old leather jacket to charity. At some point in our lives, chances are we each have tried to bargain with God.

The Jews were no different. Facing annihilation at the hands of the Assyrians and with food and water running out, they gave God an ultimatum. In her rebuke of their actions, Judith offers some sage advice: *"Listen to me, rulers of the people of Bethulia! What you have said to the people today is not right; you have even sworn and pronounced this oath between God and you, promising to surrender the town to our enemies unless the Lord turns and helps us within so many days. Who are you to put God to the test today, and to set yourselves up in the place of God in human affairs? You are putting the Almighty to the test, but you will never learn anything! You cannot plumb the depths of the human heart or understand the workings of the human mind; how do you expect to search out God, who made all these things and find out his mind or comprehend his thought? No, my brothers, do not anger the Lord our God. For if he does not choose to help us within these five days, he has power to protect us even within any time he pleases, or even to destroy us in the presence of our enemies. Do not try to bind the purposes of the Lord our God; for God is not like a human being, to be threatened, or like a mere mortal, to be won over by pleading. Therefore, while we wait for his deliverance, let us call upon him to help us, and he will hear our voice if it pleases him"* (Judith 8:11-17).

Michelangelo paid homage to several Old Testament prophets by regularly interspersing images of them about the ceiling.

**Isaiah:** An advisor to four kings of Judah, Isaiah exhorted the Israelites to mend their wicked ways or face disastrous consequences. At the same time, Isaiah spoke of promise and hope, predicting that one day a Messiah would bring comfort and joy to the chosen people:

> *For a child has been born for us, a son given to us;*
> *authority rests upon his shoulders;*
> *and he is named Wonderful Counselor, Mighty God*
> *Everlasting Father, Prince of Peace (Isaiah 9:6).*

Sound familiar? Composer George Handel used this verse from Isaiah as the basis for the lyrics to his world-famous Messiah, often heard during the Christmas season.

**Jeremiah:** A reluctant messenger of God, Jeremiah appeared to the Jews nearly 600 years before Christ. During this time the temple of Jerusalem was burned and the exile of Jews to Babylon occurred. Though mostly ignored by the people to whom he was preaching, Jeremiah did tell of God's promise to Israel: *"I will bring them back to* *this place, and I will settle them in safety. They shall be my people, and I will be their God"* (Jeremiah 32:37-38).

**Ezekiel:** Following Jeremiah, Ezekiel had the unenviable task of proclaiming God's message on the hostile streets of Babylon. In the Book of Ezekiel one will find the phrase *"they shall know that I am the Lord"* more than 60 times. God's message to his people was one of condemnation and consolation, rebuke and restoration.

**Daniel:** In 539 BC, Babylon fell to Cyrus the Great of Persia. As an advisor to the Persian ruler, Daniel may have influenced his decision to allow the Jews to leave Babylon and return to Jerusalem. A messenger of God, Daniel is best known for surviving being thrown into the lions' den.

**Joel:** Joel's message is simple. Referring to a recent locust plague, Joel likens the desolation of the land to the end of days. However, he offers hope via sincere repentance.

**Jonah:** In another short book, Jonah delivers a literary piece, likening his trials as being in the belly of a great fish, thought by some to be a whale. Evangelists Matthew and Luke quote Jesus as referring to Jonah, citing parallels between Jonah's three days in the fish and Jesus' three days in the ground after he dies. Jonah's utterance, *"Out of the belly of Sheol I cried"* (Jonah 2:2) is considered to be a reference to Christ's time in the underworld before his resurrection.

**Zechariah:** The prophet Zechariah writes about the Jews rebuilding the temple after their return from Babylonian exile. Much of his book concerns Messianic prophecies and as such influenced the New Testament Book of Revelation.

☉ ☉ ☉

Michelangelo portrayed a number of the ancestors of Jesus. Of all Christ's ancestors adorning the Sistine Chapel, Solomon is the most famous, known far and wide for his wisdom. From the first book of Kings comes this famous account:

> Later two women who were prostitutes came to the king, and stood before him. The one woman said, "Please, my lord, this woman and I live in the same house; and I gave birth while she was in the house. Then on the third day after I gave birth, this woman also gave birth. We were together; no one was with us in the house, only the two of us were in the house. Then this woman's son died in the night, because she lay on him. She got up in the middle of the night and took my son from beside me, while your servant slept. She laid him at her breast, and laid her dead son at my breast. When I rose in the morning to nurse my son, I saw that he was dead; but when I looked at him closely in the morning, clearly it was not the son I had borne."
>
> But the other woman said, "No, the living son is mine, and the dead son is yours." The first said, "No, the dead son is yours, and the living son is mine."
>
> So they argued before the king....
>
> So the king said, "Bring me a sword," and they brought a sword before the king. The king said, "Divide the living boy in two; then give half to the one and half to the other."
>
> But the woman whose son was alive said to the king — because compassion for her son burned within her — "Please, my lord, give her the living boy; certainly do not kill him!"

*The other said, "It shall be neither mine nor yours; divide it."*

*Then the king responded, "Give the first woman the living boy; do not kill him. She is his mother."*

*All Israel heard of the judgment that the king had rendered; and they stood in awe of the king, because they perceived that the wisdom of God was in him, to execute justice* (1 Kings 3:16-22, 24-28).

Solomon was not wise of his own accord; his wisdom came from God, just as all our talents are gifts from above. This holds true whether we have a gift with a three wood or a violin, are able to putt with unerring accuracy or are able to heal through medicine, are able chip well from 50 yards or teach 50 second graders how to write.

As for the walls of the Sistine Chapel, the most dominant image by Michelangelo is of the Last Judgment, where souls of the dead rise to face the wrath of Almighty God, reflecting the artist's belief that suffering played a large part in salvation. Perpendicular to this masterpiece are two walls with six paintings each that show parallel episodes from the lives of Moses and Jesus, all painted by some of the greatest artists of the fifteenth and sixteenth centuries. Among the frescoes are the Baptism of Christ in the Jordan by Perugino, the Temptation of Christ by Botticelli, the Calling of Saint Peter and Saint Andrew by Ghirlandaio, and the Sermon on Mount by Rosselli. The latter represents some of Christ's most heartfelt and poetic instruction:

*"Blessed are the poor in spirit,*
*for theirs is the kingdom of heaven.*
*Blessed are those who mourn,*
*for they will be comforted.*
*Blessed are the meek,*
*for they will inherit the earth.*
*Blessed are those who hunger and thirst*
 *for righteousness,*
*for they will be filled.*
*Blessed are the merciful,*
*for they will receive mercy.*
*Blessed are the pure in heart,*
*for they will see God.*
*Blessed are the peacemakers,*
*for they will be called children of God.*
*Blessed are those who are persecuted*
 *for righteousness' sake,*
*for theirs is the kingdom of heaven"* (Matthew 5:3-10).

The beauty of the beatitudes is that they speak, not only to different people, but also to the different parts of us all. At different points in our lives each of us has been gentle, forgiving or has mourned. For those times in our lives when we are less Christ-like than we'd like to be, the beatitudes serve as an inspirational call, stating how we ought to conduct ourselves, and the rewards for doing so.

From scenes of Creation to the Last Judgment, one would expect such sublime imagery in the papal chapel just as, upon viewing the evocative artwork, one would expect to be suitably moved in prayer and contemplation over humankind's sinfulness, Jesus' supreme sacrifice, and God's forgiveness and absolute love. What is quite surprising, however, is that a golf course along the Pacific Ocean in Pebble Beach, California would be the inspiration for such a discussion. But then God, indeed, works in mysterious ways.

SIXTEENTH HOLE
# Miracles of Golf and God

Cypress Point Club at Pebble Beach leaves viewers in awe with each new vista. Hole sixteen is one such majestic example. Tee and green are separated by 200 yards of surging sea crashing onto the craggy shoreline; ice plant and rough frame the hole. Beyond, the Pacific Ocean stretches to the horizon. Too bad one has to ruin this glorious moment by having to risk losing a half-dozen balls playing the hole. While a 200-yard iron is not intimidating in and of itself, having to loft one in the midst of saltwater spray and wind adds significantly more pressure to the shot. Worse still, the target of such an iron is a green protected fore and aft (to use terms of the sea) by sand traps near the color of the white foam of the waves below. Successfully reaching the green is cause for great celebration and much relief. Taking in the beauty that surrounds the hole is cause for great reflection and much gratitude.

Another great sixteenth is at Merion Golf Club in Ardmore, Pennsylvania. Originally built as a cricket, croquet and lawn tennis club, Merion joined the golfing fraternity in September 1912. Designed by Hugh Wilson, the suburban Philadelphia course is small by today's standards but rich with tradition. Prior to his work on Merion, Wilson spent seven months in Great Britain researching the great courses of Scotland and England. Two features at the Pennsylvania course owe their influence to this trip: the triangular wicker baskets that sit atop the flagsticks in lieu of flags, and the steep Scottish-style bunkers called "the white faces of Merion."[1]

Merion also played a part in giving golf one of its most popular terms. In 1930, Bobby Jones captured the U.S. Amateur at Merion East. Having already earned the British Amateur, the Open Championship

(British Open) and U.S. Open earlier in the year, Jones had now claimed the fourth of the four most prestigious tournaments of the day. In seeking to define the accomplishment, Atlanta newsman O.B. Keeler referred to the quartet of victories as the Grand Slam.[2] Today the term is associated with the winning of the four major tournaments: Masters, U. S. Open, British Open and PGA Championship.

Ben Hogan and Lee Trevino were the beneficiaries of playoff favors at Merion. In 1950, Hogan captured the U.S. Open, rallying to tie for the lead on the last day and going on to win an 18-hole playoff. Twenty-one years later, Trevino bested Jack Nicklaus 68 to 71 in their Open playoff.

One of Merion's notable holes, and one of the more unique holes in all of golf, is number sixteen. Known as The Quarry,[3] the sixteenth is a 448-yard, par 4 that crosses, not surprisingly, a steep quarry some 300 yards from the tee. Other courses tout hazards where one is faced with steep bunkers or deep creeks. Few if any have one where a golfer nearly has to repel down a limestone face into waist high-brambles and sand. Talk about landing in the rough! The less inclined mountaineering players have the option of taking a more circumspect route to the green by way of a looping fairway detour to the far right of said hazard. Such an approach, while much safer, inevitably adds another stroke to the hole. Even those who dare try to carry the quarry must do so with gusto, for two deep bunkers and a steep slope await second shots that don't quite make the green. Just on Merion's sixteenth alone, one needs a grand slam of a second shot for a, well, a shot at par.

Six years after Merion opened, Oakland Hills South came into being with quite a pedigree. Renowned architect Donald Ross designed the Bloomfield Hills, Michigan, course, and its first club pro was a gentleman by the name of Walter Hagen, already a U.S. Open winner. (Think of Jack Nicklaus designing a world-class course today with Tiger Woods as the club pro.) Oakland Hills has played host to a number of U.S. Open and PGA championships. Victors include U.S. Open winners Ben Hogan (1951), Gene Littler (1961), Andy North (1985), and Steve Jones (1996), and PGA champs Gary Player (1972) and David Graham (1979). A pair of by then elder statesmen captured the U.S. Senior Open at Oakland Hills—Arnold Palmer (1981) and Jack Nicklaus (1991).

If the willows don't make one weep, the water often will.

It was the 1951 U.S. Open that gave Oakland Hills its nickname of The Monster. Hogan took home the title with a final score of 287, including a final round 67. Said a relived champion, "I'm glad I brought this course, this monster, to its knees."[4] Monster indeed. In 1985, Open winner Andy North was the only participant to produce a four-day total under par.

Oakland Hills' signature hole, and one that helps contribute to so many over pars, is number sixteen, a par 4, 406-yarder with a dogleg that angles sharply to the right. A large pond framed by giant willow trees protects the front and right side of the green. If the willows don't make one weep, the water often will. Adding further consternation are four bunkers at the rear of the green to frustrate anyone hoping to launch their iron far over the pond and trees. Should one gain the green in two, there is still a putting surface with which to contend, a wide shallow affair with a ridge running front to back. The entire scene is serene until one has to swing a club.

It was at Oakland Hills, during the 1972 PGA Championship, that Gary Player lofted an incredible, some would say a miraculous shot, to propel him to victory. His drive landed in the right rough in a position where the weeping willows blocked what would have been a simple approach shot to the green. Player needed his next shot to be hit high enough to overcome the willows. Normally this would not be a problem. However, the tall sentinels stood guard in front of a water hazard, which in turn guarded the green. So not only would the South African need to carry over the top of the tree, he'd have to carry over the water. Hit too low and the willow wouldn't be the only one weeping. Hit too short and the water hazard would cause tears of its own. Hit too far and the ball would carry over the green. Any misplay would no doubt resort in a bogey or worse in this the third to the last hole of the tournament. "Or worse" included possibly losing the tournament. That's a lot to be riding on a single 9-iron shot. Player's shot was near perfect. He cleared the trees, carried the water, and landed four feet from the cup. One putt later, he had the birdie that would help earn him a one-stroke victory and his second PGA championship.

Webster defines a "miracle" as a wonder or marvel; an effect or extraordinary event in the physical world that surpasses all known human or natural powers and is ascribed to a supernatural cause; and such an effect or event manifesting or considered a work of God.

For wonders or marvels, golf offers examples of those weekly. You can view incredible shots on the course regularly during the "Top Ten Plays" installment on ESPN's *Sports Center*. Or check out the many Tiger Woods entries on YouTube.

Now if you take the position that a miracle is a heretofore impossible event that occurs once, never to be repeated again, then golf has its fair share of miraculous events. Byron Nelson won a phenomenal 18 tour events in 1945, including 11 in a row. Most golfers would consider that an outstanding career. Chances are good that Lord Byron's twelve-month accomplishment will never be equaled, and therefore could be considered miraculous.

The same could be said of Tiger Woods' four major tournament wins in a row in 2001 and 2002, Sam Snead's career total of 82 PGA tour victories, or Jack Nicklaus' 18 major championships. Of course, records are made to be broken. And if anyone has a chance at Slammin' Sammy's 82 or the Golden Bear's 18, it would be Woods. As of June 2008 El Tigre has posted 65 tour victories and 14 major championships.

Our third definition of miracle is an effect or event manifesting or considered a work of God. These events fall roughly into two areas: The major work of God, eternal and infinite, the supreme creator of all that is; and the minor work of God, who rested on the seventh day to watch golf, which might explain a number of miraculous shots over the years on courses around the world.

Augusta National has been home to several incredible displays of shot-making. At hole eleven during the second sudden death playoff hole of the 1987 Masters, Larry Mize defeated Greg Norman with a remarkable 140-foot pitch that found nothing but the bottom of the cup.[6] A year later, on the eighteenth during the final round, with the outcome of the Masters hanging in the balance, Sandy Lyle found himself in a fairway bunker. One miraculous 145-yard, 7-iron shot later, Lyle was on the green for a birdie and a green jacket.[7]

Norman was the victim of yet another amazing grace. At the eighteenth at Inverness, Bob Tway holed his greenside bunker shot for a birdie, a one-stroke victory over the Shark, and the 1986 PGA Championship. Watch the clip on YouTube and you can see Tway literally jumping for joy.[8]

In 1972 at Pebble Beach, Jack Nicklaus defied Mother Nature. The stage was the U.S. Open. Nicklaus had a one shot lead over Lee Trevino and Kermit Zarley at the start of the final round. As he was about to strike his one-iron on the par 3, 178-yard seventeenth, a sudden gust of wind off the ocean forced the clubface more closed than the Golden Bear intended. In a split second's time, Nicklaus was able to correct in mid-swing right before impact. The shot defied the wind to hit the flagstick and land within six inches of the cup.[9] The ensuing birdie helped Nicklaus win his thirteenth major championship, tying Bobby Jones for the then most ever.

For the Golden Bear, what Pebble Beach giveth, the same course taketh away. At the same seventeenth hole ten years later, again during the final round, Tom Watson hit his two-iron into some nasty fescue that guarded the hourglass-shaped putting surface. Most, including Nicklaus who sat in the clubhouse with the lead, thought Watson would be extremely lucky to get his ball within five to seven feet of the hole. Yet the redhead's carefully considered shot found the hole in one of golf's most legendary moments.[10] No wonder around Pebble

Beach, Tom Terrific's effort is known simply as The Shot.[11] Watson's chip became all the more important because it gave him the 1982 U.S. Open title.

A good many sports fans are familiar with baseball's Shot Heard 'Round the World—Bobby Thomson's walk off home run in the 1951 National League playoff game between the Brooklyn Dodgers and Thomson's New York Giants. What people may not know is that golf has its own, earlier version of the SHRTW. At the fifteenth hole during 1935 Masters, Gene Sarazen's drive left him in a bad lie, his ball sitting low in the grass at the front edge of a divot. After selecting a four-wood, Sarazen walloped his ball 235 yards, the dimpled orb soaring into the air. Upon descent, the ball reached the edge of the green, bounced twice, and rolled into the hole for a double eagle.[12] That's right, a double eagle. Sarazen scored a miraculous two on the 485-yard, par 5, helping him to a share of the lead after regulation play. The next day, Sarazen was Masters champion.

What could a shot that traveled further than the length of two football fields to land in a hole 4.25 inches in diameter be but a miracle? Well, a true miracle, that is a Miracle, is heaven sent, by God through the Spirit. A Miracle is a message from on high that there is an awe-inducing power greater than even an incredible golf shot—a force of goodness and love that calls us all to those very same qualities that reside deep within us.

In order that we might believe that he is God and man, paradoxically 100 percent divine and 100 percent human, Jesus performed signs throughout his ministry to authenticate his mission.

As one follows Mark's account of Jesus' ministry, the reader encounters miracle after miracle. Jesus casts out an unclean spirit, demons, and a deaf and dumb spirit, demonstrating his power over the forces of evil. Christ heals Peter's mother-in-law, a paralyzed man, a man with a withered hand, and a woman with a hemorrhage, showing power over sickness. The Lord calms a storm, walks on water, and withers a fig tree, revealing power over nature. He raises Jairus' daughter exhibiting power over death. The Son of God feeds 5,000 on one occasion and 4,000 on another, displaying power to provide sustenance. The Word of God heals a deaf mute and two blind men on different occasions, indicating power over sight and sound. How's that for a resume?

Jesus' miracles were not just a display of the divine. They were teaching tools, albeit quite dramatic ones. By way of example, look at the miracle of the hemorrhaging woman and the raising of Jairus' daughter:

> When Jesus had crossed again in the boat to the other side, a great crowd gathered around him; and he was by the sea. Then one of the leaders of the synagogue named Jairus came and, when he saw him, fell at his feet and begged him repeatedly, "My little daughter is at the point of death. Come and lay your hands on her, so that she made be made well, and live." So he went with him.
>
> And a large crowd followed him and pressed in on him. Now there was a woman who had been suffering from hemorrhages for twelve years. She had endured much under many physicians, and had spent all that she had; and she was no better, but rather grew worse. She had heard about Jesus, and came up behind him

in the crowd and touched his cloak, for she said, "If I but touch his clothes, I will be made well." Immediately her hemorrhage stopped; and she felt in her body that she was healed of her disease.

Immediately aware that power had gone forth from him, Jesus turned about in the crowd and said, "Who touched my clothes?" And his disciples said to him, " You see the crowd pressing in on you; how can you say, 'Who touched me?'" He looked all around to see who had done it. But the woman knowing what had happened to her, came in fear and trembling, fell down before him, and told him the whole truth. "Daughter, your faith has made you well; go in peace, and be healed of your disease."

While he was still speaking, some people came from the leader's house to say, "Your daughter is dead. Why trouble the teacher any further?" But overhearing what they said, Jesus said to the leader of the synagogue, "Do not fear, only believe." He allowed no one to follow him except Peter, James, and John, the brother of James. When they came to the house of the leader of the synagogue, he saw a commotion, people weeping and wailing loudly. When he had entered, he said to them, "Why do you make a commotion and weep? The child is not dead but sleeping." And they laughed at him. Then he put them all outside, and took the child's father and mother and those who were with him, and went in where the child was. He took her by the hand and said to her, "Talitha cum," which means, "Little girl, get up!" And immediately the girl got up and began to walk about (she was twelve years of age). At this they were overcome with amazement (Mark 5:21-42).

Jesus' actions spoke volumes. He availed himself to the powerful and powerless alike. Christ showed that he didn't play favorites. His words, his compassion, were available to anyone and everyone. He responded, loved even, indiscriminately and absolutely. In this case, a ruler who possessed status, access and power was no different than an unknown and unclean--therefore likely ostracized--woman in a patriarchal society. Each was granted an audience with the Lord. He listened to both, empathized with their respective troubles, came to their aid. Both were equal in his eyes.

As we've come to expect from Jesus, there was a lesson revealed in how he responded. One could make the case that the ruler had approached Christ formally and therefore had a right to his time. Yet, the Lord diverted his attention from the man to minister to the afflicted woman. In effect, Jesus said that in our day-to-day activities, as we respond to our various duties and responsibilities, we are not to forget or ignore the poor, the powerless, the foreigner, the sick. Not only that, an argument could be made that by Jesus' example we are to take care of the neglected and oppressed first before anything else.

Through his works, however, Jesus was both accepted and rejected. There were some Jews and Gentiles who truly believed that Jesus was the Messiah in their midst. There were considerably more who were expecting a political or military savior to rescue them from Roman persecution. The religious leaders of the day, feeling their own sense of power threatened, denounced Jesus as a heretic.

In the Gospel of John, the author records seven signs (seven being the biblical mythical number of plenty). Each of these miracles—

including the changing of water into wine, multiplying the loaves and fish, and walking on water—helped to further indicate Christ's divinity and substantiate his being the Messiah. But the last of John's seven recorded signs is by far the most dramatic and impressive—the raising of Lazarus from the dead:

> *When Jesus arrived, he found that Lazarus had already been in the tomb for four days.... When Martha heard that Jesus was coming, she went and met him, while Mary stayed at home. Martha said to Jesus, "Lord, if you had been here, my brother would not have died. But even now I know that God will give you whatever you ask of him."*
>
> *Then Jesus, again greatly disturbed, came to the tomb. It was a cave, and a stone was lying against it.*
>
> *Jesus said, "Take away the stone." Martha, the sister of the dead man, said to him, "Lord, already there is a stench because he has been dead for four days." Jesus said to her, "Did I not tell you that if you believed, you would see the glory of God?" So they took away the stone. And Jesus looked upwards and said, "Father, I thank you for having heard me. I knew that you always hear me, but I have said this for the sake of the crowd standing here, so that they may believe that you sent me." When he had said this, he cried with a loud voice, "Lazarus, come out!" The dead man came out, his hands and feet bound with strips of cloth, and his face wrapped in a cloth. Jesus said to them, "Unbind him, and let him go." (John 11:17, 20-22, 38-44).*

Talk about marvels and wonders. Here Jesus accomplished the unfathomable—raising a man from the dead. In so doing, Christ revealed heartfelt emotion. He was so overcome he groaned. John says, *"Jesus began to weep. So the Jews said, 'See how he loved him!'"* (John 11:35-36). They may have been tears of grief that Christ wept for his friend and his sisters. They may have been tears of sadness that, as a human, Lazarus would have to face death again. Perhaps Jesus was anticipating his own dying. Or the fact that it had come to this: that after all the words he had preached and works he had performed, there were still those who doubted his ministry and mission.

Regardless, just as he had done time and again, Jesus called

upon the love of his Father and performed the miracle of miracles. True, modern medicine has allowed doctors to resuscitate victims who have been technically dead in that their hearts had stopped beating. But Lazarus had been

pronounced dead, wrapped in grave-clothes, and been entombed for four days! Jesus had demonstrated power over nature, the elements, sickness, handicaps, and now death itself. The stage was set for his own death, and the overcoming of it by his own resurrection.

When Jesus cured a man who was lame, Jesus asked his critics which was easier, to forgive a paralytic of his sins or to say arise and walk? Similarly, if we have doubts of faith, if we question whether Jesus walked on water or turned water into wine, perhaps we should consider golf. After all, if Larry Mize can hole out a 140-foot pitch shot to win the Masters, Tom Watson can successfully sink "The Shot" at Pebble Beach to capture the U.S. Open, and Gene Sarazen can record a double eagle from nearly a different time zone at Augusta, what golfer can say that miracles can't happen?

So next time we face a difficult shot on the course, or a difficult period in the course of our lives, remember the words of Jesus: *"Do not fear, only believe"* (Mark 5:36).

Believe in what? In the death and resurrection of Christ. In his love and mercy. In the forgiveness of sins. In life everlasting.

# Golf's Greatest

Nearing the completion of the back nine, golf courses often save their best, and most challenging, holes for last. Carnoustie's seventeenth is one such example. Called the Island Hole,[1] this par 4, 443-yarder is really only a semi-island, though for as many players who have lost balls in the water this distinction is far from comforting. Giving the hole its character is the Billy Burn, a serpentine waterway that starts on the right hand side of the fairway, meanders up toward the tee area then down the left hand side and ever so gradually cuts diagonally across back to the right, in effect cutting the fairway in two, creating an "island" of a landing area. Those persuaded to hit long and cross the burn at its shortest point on the left face the prospect of landing in the rough or a small sand trap. Those playing safe on the right face a much longer approach to the green. Speaking of which, any approach to the putting area needs to be true, for bunkers and gorse lie waiting for the wayward shot. Billy Burn is a snake in the grass of the golfing kind. And nothing well comes to those whose balls find the burn.

For a true Island Green, travel to the Tournament Players Club at Sawgrass in Ponte Vedra Beach, Florida. There, on the seventeenth hole, is Pete Dye's world-famous creation designed to test players' mettle as well as metal, or at least wedges. At 132 yards, this is one of the shortest par 3s around, but also one of the most difficult. Situated in a large lagoon lies an emerald isle, a 78-foot long green surround by a fringe of rough and water, water everywhere. Except for a thin grass walkway to the putting surface, the entire green is an island. Though a mere wedge shot for most professionals, the effort from the tee to green can be unnerving. In 2007 alone, at the TPC Championship, the world's best players deposited 50 balls in the drink. Of course, this is a mere fraction of the more than 100,000 fished out every year, compliments of players who come up too short, left, right, or far with their tee shots.

While Carnoustie and Sawgrass create their challenges on the seventeenth with water, Saint Andrews Old accomplishes the same with good ol' terra firma. Called the Road Hole,[2] this 460-yard, par 4 borders the town of Saint Andrews at the green. In fact the far end of the putting surface nestles up to an old turnpike road on the fringe of town, a road by the way that is in play, as is the stone wall behind it. Road and wall are of a concern because the green itself is quite wide and shallow, running parallel to the unusual hazards. One may be tempted to lay up short of the green to avoid asphalt and stone. However, doing so invites introduction to one of the most notorious landmarks in all of golf, the Road Bunker. This cavernous, sheer-faced trap is situated so perfectly, so maliciously, as to gobble up many a ball and player attempting to avoid the road. Conversely, the road and wall are so aligned with the green that they wreak havoc with any shot that carries long to avoid the Road Bunker. Such was the case with a Tom Watson shot with a little too much oomph, costing him the 1984 British Open championship.[3]

Sun setting against the old brick buildings of the town and undulating green of the fairway make for a picture-postcard view. Unless of course the only thing you can see is the sheer sod wall of the Road Bunker with no escape in sight. Anyone playing number seventeen at Saint Andrews hopes the road, and Road Bunker, are less traveled, at least by them.

In the Gospel of Luke a road comes into play with dramatic and exciting results. The road in question is the one to Emmaus:

> *Now on the same day two of them were going to a village called Emmaus, about seven miles from Jerusalem, and talking with each other about all these things that had happened. While they were talking and discussing, Jesus himself came near and went with them, but their eyes were kept from recognizing him. And he said to them, "What are you discussing with each other as you walk along?" They stood still, looking sad. Then one of them, whose name was Cleopas, answered him, "Are you the only stranger in Jerusalem who does not know these things that have taken place there in these days?" He asked them, "What things?" They replied, "The things about Jesus of Nazareth, who was a prophet mighty in deed and word before God and all the people, and how our chief priests and leaders handed him over to be condemned to death and crucified him. But we had hope that he was the one to redeem Israel. Yes, and besides all this, it is now the third day since these things took place. Moreover, some women of our group astounded us. They were at the tomb early this morning, and when they did not find his body there, they came back and told us that they had indeed seen a vision of angels who said that he was alive. Some of those who were with us went to the tomb and found it just as the women had said; but they did not see him." Then he said to them, "Oh, how foolish you are, and how slow of heart to believe all that the prophets have declared! Was it not necessary that the Messiah suffer these things and then enter into his glory?" Then beginning with Moses and all the prophets, he interpreted to them the things*

*about himself in all the scriptures.*

*As they came near the village to which they were going, he walked ahead as if he were going on. But they urged him strongly, saying, "Stay with us, because it is almost evening and the day is now nearly over." So he went in to stay with them. When he was at table with them, he took bread, blessed and broke it, and gave it to them. Then their eyes were opened, and they recognized him; and he vanished from their sight. They said to each other, "Were not our hearts burning within us while he was talking to us on the road, while he was opening the scriptures to us?" That same hour they got up and returned to Jerusalem; and they found the eleven and their companions gathered together. They were saying, "The Lord has risen indeed, and he has appeared to Simon!" Then they told what had happened on the road, and how he had been made known to them in the breaking of the bread* (Luke 24:13-35).

Emmaus was about seven miles from Jerusalem, and seven is the biblical number of plenty. This distance may be Luke's way of hinting that what happened in Jerusalem—the trial, condemnation, crucifixion and death of Christ—is extremely far removed from what would be revealed at Emmaus. That is, Jesus rose from the dead, having conquered sin in the process and made true all that had been prophesied about the Son of God.

Think of how upset or depressed Tom Watson must have been on seventeen at Saint Andrews after watching his chance at the 1984 British Open be stonewalled. Conversely, imagine the elation he must have felt at the seventeenth at Carnoustie on the final round in 1974 en route to his first British Open Championship. For a golfer, no doubt winning the Open would place third only to their wedding and the birth of their children. These emotions would have paled in comparison to those of Cleopas and colleague on the road to Emmaus. Their hopes had been raised that Jesus was the Messiah, the Promised One, David's heir who would lead the Israelites from captivity to their rightful place as the chosen people of God. To see the Lord humiliated, beaten and nailed to a trec to die in the midday sun surely would have crushed their spirits, and those of all the disciples. Then to learn that all that the Lord had proclaimed and foretold had come to be, no wonder their hearts burned with fervor and excitement!

As should ours.

Some of the greatest holes and moments in all of golf have been discussed in these pages. At this point, you might ask the question: Well, then, who is the greatest golfer of all time? Such a query makes for prolonged and sometimes heated conversations at the nineteenth hole on golf courses everywhere. What with statistics covering everything from career victories to putting accuracy, fans and enthusiasts, players and scribes all have their opinion as to who should be pronounced Number One. This should come as no surprise.

Even the apostles themselves jockeyed for top billing:

> *James and John, the sons of Zebedee, came forward to him*
> *and said to him, "Teacher, we want you to do for us whatever*
> *we ask of you."*
>
> *And he said to them, "What is it you want me to do for*
> *you?"*
>
> *And they said to him, "Grant us to sit, one at your right*
> *hand, and one at your left, in your glory"* (Mark 10:35-37).
>
> *When the ten heard it, they were angry with the two*
> *brothers* (Matthew 20:24).

Perhaps the other apostles were embarrassed at the brothers' effrontery. But it's more likely that they themselves wanted the exalted positions next to Jesus. After all, Luke did report: *"A dispute also arose among them as to which one of them was to be regarded as the greatest"* (Luke 22:24).

All of which just goes to show that whether twelve apostles gather, or a dozen sportswriters, eventually talk is going to come around to who's Number One. In the golf world at least, a case can be made for several of the game's masters.

With golf first played in Great Britain, it is from there that the first great golfers came. Perhaps taking their cue from the Blessed Trinity came the Great Triumvirate of James Braid, John Henry Taylor and Harry Vardon. In the twenty years between 1894 and 1913, one of the trio won the Open Championship sixteen times. Scotsman Braid and Englishman Taylor each won five times. Braid even went on to help design Carnoustie for the 1926 Open. Vardon, a Brit, won the Open a record six times, along with the 1920 U.S. Open. He won 62 tournaments in all and popularized the grip that bears him name, where the little finger of the trailing or lower hand on the club locks between the index and middle fingers of the lead or upper hand. That wasn't Vardon's only contribution to the game. He was the first links-man to ever wear knickers. Until then, proper English golfers played in trousers, shirt, tie and buttoned up jacket. As a tribute to his skill, the PGA awards the Vardon Trophy annually to the player on tour with the lowest adjusted scoring average.

One man may very well be responsible for introducing golf to America. What Babe Ruth was to baseball, Bobby Jones was to golf. As major championships were counted in his day, he collected thirteen, including four U.S. Opens and three British Opens. In 1926 he became the first ever to win The Double—both the U.S. and British opens in the same year. Doing himself two better, Jones became the only player to win the four majors of the day in the same year. In 1930 in an incredible display of athleticism, he captured the U.S. Open, the British Open, the U.S. Amateur and British Amateur. A man of many talents, Jones retired from golf at the seemingly young age of twenty-eight. With a degree in mechanical engineering from Georgia (not to mention English Literature from Harvard and Law from Emory University), Jones co-designed Augusta National with architect Alister MacKenzie, and was one of the founders of the Masters Tournament. In 1948, he fell victim to syringomyelia, leaving him paralyzed and having to use a wheelchair. He passed away in 1971. Today his name is still synonymous with the Grand Slam. The USGA has named its annual sportsmanship award The Bobby Jones Award.[4]

Two players who helped popularize the game stateside and turn it into a professional sport were Walter Hagen and Gene Sarazen. Hagen was born in 1892, and in 1914, while in his early twenties, he captured the first of his eleven majors, the U.S. Open, an event he was also to win five years later. In 1922, he became the first American to win the Open Championship. A master at hitting a ball, Hagen once cancelled a tryout with baseball's Philadelphia Phillies to play in a golf tournament (which he won).[5] In addition to his two U.S. Open victories, Hagen owns four British Open championships as well a record-tying five PGA wins. As consistent a performer as there was in the sport, Hagen captured at least one major annually eight times in nine years from 1921 to 1929.

Born in 1902, Gene Sarazen is recognized for two notable accomplishments. He is one of only five players (along with Ben Hogan, Gary Player, Jack Nicklaus and Tiger Woods) to have captured each of the four majors at least once. Sarazen's Career Slam breaks down this way: PGA in 1922, 1923 and 1933; British Open in 1932, Masters in 1935, and U.S. Open in 1922 and 1932. Helping him win the Open Championship was a club of his own invention—a sand iron—that is now known as a sand wedge and is a staple in golf bags everywhere. As icing on a remarkable career cake, at the age of 73, Sarazen scored a hole in one during the 1973 British Open at Royal Troon.[6]

Another of golf's blessed trinities is the threesome of Ben Hogan, Byron Nelson and Sam Snead. Remarkably, these three gentlemen were born within six months of each other in 1912,[7] with Hogan and Snead entering the world two weeks apart. As if this weren't coincidence enough, at the age of 14, Nelson defeated a fellow caddie by the name of Ben Hogan in an early tournament.[8]

In 1930, Hogan first turned pro. In what must be an inspiration to beginning golfers everywhere, he battled a hook early in his career. He did not win his first tournament until nine years later, going broke more than once in the intervening years. However, through meticulous practice, Hogan honed his swing so as to become the paragon of professionals. He is one of only five golfers to have won each major tournament at least once. His career was nearly derailed by an auto accident. But less than a year after spending two months in a hospital he won the 1950 U.S. Open, an event he captured four times.[9]

Hogan is one of only five golfers to have won each major tournament at least once.

Byron Nelson set a record that may never be broken, winning eighteen tournaments in 1945, including an unheard of eleven in a row. A look at that magical year resembles a road trip, compliments of Rand-McNally. Among other places, Nelson captured events in Phoenix, Corpus Christi, New Orleans, Miami, Charlotte, Greensboro, Durham, Atlanta, Montreal, Philadelphia, Chicago, Knoxville, Esmeralda and Seattle.[10] Included in his victory tour was a win at the PGA Championship in Dayton. In addition to that PGA, he also won the event in 1940, as well as the 1937 and 1942 Masters and the 1939 U.S. Open.

As for Slammin' Sammy Snead, he captured seven majors, the U.S. Open being the only one to escape him. Along the way, Snead won 82 PGA tournaments. After Nelson won his two Masters in six years before World War II, one would have thought that after the war Augusta had become the private backyard of Snead and Hogan.

Ever the gentlemen, the pair alternated victories in five of six years, repeatedly giving each other a turn at the top:

| 1949 | Snead |
| 1951 | Hogan |
| 1952 | Snead |
| 1953 | Hogan |
| 1954 | Snead |

Hogan, Nelson and Snead didn't just master the Masters. The three played King of the Green with the PGA Championship too. In the span of 11 years from 1940 through 1951 (the event was cancelled in 1943 due to the war), these "triplets" took the PGA seven times:

| 1940 | Nelson |
| 1942 | Snead |
| 1945 | Nelson |
| 1946 | Hogan |
| 1948 | Hogan |
| 1949 | Snead |
| 1951 | Snead |

In the late 1950s and 1960s, yet another trio captured the collective imagination of golf aficionados and sports fans everywhere. Gary Player, Arnold Palmer and Jack Nicklaus pretty much owned golf during those years. Their highly competitive matches, charismatic personalities and phenomenal skills helped usher golf into the age of television. Player and Nicklaus are members of the select Career Slam fraternity, while Palmer, by virtue of his good looks and aggressive playing style, amassed legions of followers, on the course and off, known as Arnie's Army.

Palmer claimed seven major championships, including four Masters. Player did Palmer two better, winning nine majors, including three Masters and three PGAs. Nicklaus did Player two better, as in two times better, winning 18 majors. Nicklaus' triumphs are so arrayed that he is a Career Slam winner three times. The Golden Bear won 6 Masters, 5 PGAs, 4 U.S. Opens, 3 British Opens, two turtledoves and a partridge in a pear tree.

To give an idea of how The Big Three ruled the game for years at a time, take a look at how they traded major tournament victories amongst themselves:

| MASTERS | | U.S. OPEN | | PGA | |
|---------|---------|-----------|----------|------|----------|
| 1958 | Palmer | 1960 | Palmer | 1962 | Player |
| 1960 | Palmer | 1962 | Nicklaus | 1963 | Nicklaus |
| 1961 | Player | 1965 | Player | 1971 | Nicklaus |
| 1962 | Palmer | 1967 | Nicklaus | 1972 | Player |
| 1963 | Nicklaus | 1972 | Nicklaus | 1973 | Nicklaus |
| 1964 | Palmer | 1974 | Nicklaus | | |
| 1965 | Nicklaus | | | | |
| 1966 | Nicklaus | | | | |

Among his many distinctions, Nicklaus was also a member of still another trinity of special players. Joining Jack to rule from the late 1960s to early 1980s were Lee Trevino and Tom Watson. As mentioned earlier, the self-taught Trevino overcame an impoverished upbringing to become one of golf's most beloved players. His six majors include a pair of U.S. Opens, British Opens and PGA Championships. Watson's penchant for practicing whatever shot he thought he might need on a course was instrumental in allowing him to make "The Shot" at Pebble Beach to win the 1982 U.S. Open. In addition, he captured two Masters and five, count them five, British Open Championships, to become one of the most popular Americans to ever play across the pond. The golfing firm of Nicklaus, Trevino & Watson specialized in producing Open championships, be they the U.S. or British variety:

| U.S. OPEN | | BRITISH OPEN | |
|---|---|---|---|
| 1967 | Nicklaus | 1966 | Nicklaus |
| 1968 | Trevino | 1970 | Nicklaus |
| 1971 | Trevino | 1971 | Trevino |
| 1972 | Nicklaus | 1972 | Trevino |
| 1980 | Nicklaus | 1975 | Watson |
| 1982 | Watson | 1977 | Watson |
| | | 1978 | Nicklaus |
| | | 1980 | Watson |
| | | 1982 | Watson |
| | | 1983 | Watson |

Among contemporary ball strikers, one golfer stands club-head and shoulders above the field: Tiger Woods. A child golfing prodigy, Eldrick Tiger Woods dominated junior and amateur play, winning among other titles the U.S. Amateur Championship three times and an NCAA individual golf title. These only served as a taste for what was to come when Tiger joined the PGA tour.

In just his second year on tour, Woods not only won the 1997 Masters, he dominated the field, winning by a record twelve strokes. To put that in perspective, Woods could have had three additional bogeys in each of the four rounds and have tied for the lead. The year

2000 turned out to be an especially good year for Tiger. He captured the U.S. Open by a remarkable fifteen strokes, the British Open and his second PGA championship. The following April he won his second Masters, holding four consecutive major titles in what has become known as the Tiger Slam. As mentioned above, Jack Nicklaus has three career slams among his 18 majors. Tiger has three Career Slams among his fourteen, including four PGAs, four Masters, three British Opens and three of the U.S. variety. And if Woods has his way these numbers will continue to increase.

Major championships alone only tell part of Tiger's tale. It's how he wins that is most impressive. At one point in his career he was 31-6 in tournaments in which he led after 36 holes, 44-3 in which he led after 54 holes, and 14-0 when he entered the final round in, or with a share of, the lead.[11] To honor his alma mater, Stanford, Tiger wears his by now trademark red shirt on the days of a final round. He's appeared on the victory stand more than 60 times so dressed.

In the second round of the 2007 PGA tournament, Tiger tied a major championship scoring record, posting a 63 to take control of the tournament. He barely missed birdies on the last two holes, with his putt on eighteen circling the lip of the cup before rolling out. So close was he to breaking the course record that he gave himself a "sixty-two and a half."[12]

In a long line of remarkable shots, one of his most memorable and talked about was on the sixteenth hole at Augusta during the 2005 Masters. Named Redbud, the 170-yard par three has a large pond that separates tee from green, which slopes significantly from right to left. Woods' iron off the tee landed 30 feet away from the cup against the second cut of grass around the green, limiting his back-swing. Watch the shot on YouTube.[13] Woods chipped to a landing area on the green where his ball followed the contours of the putting surface, tracing an elongated S to the cup. As the ball rolled closer and closer to the cup, the gallery's cheering rose accordingly. At the lip of the cup, the ball paused, as if peering over the edge to judge the drop, before completing its revolution to fall into the bottom of the hole to a deafening roar. TV announcer Vern Lundquist mirrored the excitement on the course with his call: "Oh my goodness! Oh my! In your life! Have you ever seen anything like that?!"

Hagen and Hogan. Nelson and Nicklaus. Snead and Sarazen. Palmer and Player. Jones and Vardon. Not surprisingly, all were among the inaugural class of the World Golf Hall of Fame. Trevino and Watson have subsequently been elected, and a space is most assuredly reserved for Tiger Woods. All of these athletes have had incredible careers and have contributed much to the game. Depending upon the criteria, all could be considered the greatest. Most though would argue for either the Golden Bear or Tiger. However, for building a case for any player to be considered The Greatest, one should consult more than the golfing record books. One should also take a look at the Good Book.

Especially when we define greatness as Jesus does.

In responding to the qualities of greatness, Jesus said: *"Whoever wishes to be great among you must be your servant"* (Matthew 20:26).

With this in mind, the fact that Lee Trevino and Arnold Palmer served their country in the Marine Corps and Coast Guard, respectively, takes on different meaning. Bobby Jones left the game to practice law and contribute to the community. He was so kind and respectful while on the course that a sportsmanship award was named after him.

Similarly, the PGA established the Payne Stewart Award to perpetuate Stewart's respect for the traditions of the game and his commitment to the game's heritage of community support. Past winners have included Nelson, Nicklaus and Palmer.[14] In 2006 Gary Player earned the award in part for his work for the underpriviledged worldwide through the Gary Player Foundation,[15] which benefits education. In 2007, Hal Sutton was honored for his part in raising, with fellow golfers David Toms and Kelley Gibson, more than $2 million to help the victims of hurricanes Katrina and Rita in Louisiana.[16] Tiger Woods has established

Bobby Jones left the game to practice law and contribute to the community.

the Tiger Woods Foundation and the Tiger Woods Learning Center.[17] Even John Daly, despite his up and down career, has supported the Make-A-Wish Foundation, Boys & Girls Clubs and the University of Arkansas sports department.[18]

Jesus also taught his apostles: *"No one has greater love than this, to lay down one's life for one's friends"* (John 15:13). We may not realize it, but we all do this in little ways. Parents give of themselves to raise their children. Clergy give of their lives to minister to their flocks. Young people give of themselves in the service of the less fortunate.

Christ demands of us that we serve others, that we give of ourselves, of our livelihoods, of our lives to those near and far. We do what we can, but we may have the potential to do more.

To live a good life, it's not enough to excel in our profession (even if that profession is as a professional golfer). We must also strive to excel as human beings. To hold others with respect, care, service and love. As Jesus said: *For what will it profit them if they gain the whole world but forfeit their life?* (Matthew 16:26).

As we play through the rounds of life, as much if not more effort should be devoted to service as success, kindness as well as kudos, love as well as laurels. Doing so makes all winners in God's eyes.

# Valley of Sin, Death on a Cross

Golf course architects, after providing equal parts pleasure and pain, tease and torture, beauty and beasts for seventeen holes, desire to leave players with one last remarkable moment from which to remember their works of art. Nowhere is this more true than on the final hole at Pebble Beach. Such splendor should be savored. Perhaps that's why course designers Jack Neville, Douglas Grant and H. Chandler Egan chose to let golfers linger on a closing hole that measures 548 yards for its par five. Resembling the inside curve of a banana, the left side of the entire hole has as its border a sweeping arc of the Pacific Ocean. One can choose to play fairway as it lies safely or cut across the water in search of par or bird. Though beware, a wayward drive left will land upon the rocky beach or in the world's largest water hazard. That's not to say that the right hand play is not without its own concerns. Chief among them are a sandy bunker and small groups of cypress trees. Steep bunkers on the left and right of the green further complicate matters. Whether one plays left or right, aggressive or safe, the vista is heaven sent. Not only do sea and sky provide breathtaking views but also players are often cheered by patrons of the ocean-side gallery, namely sea otters, seals or dolphins, golfing fans all.

A sweeping dogleg left marks the 450-yard, par 4 finale at Winged Foot West. Long and narrow, the hole requires a precise drive in order to set up a mid-iron to a rather tricky green. An undulating putting surface runs extremely quick from back to front. Anything short that lands on the front ridge of the green has a tendency to roll back down the slope. The final hole on the course, it has been given for its moniker an appropriate biblical counterpart—Revelation, the last book of the Bible.

Next, what better place to end a tour of courses than in the country where golf began? Saint Andrews, host to more British Open championships than any other course in the rotation, offers a par 4, 357-yard effort to close its round. A road traversing the fairway is in play, and should a ball land there, from there it must be played. From the tee, players are advised to drive straight for the R&A clock tower of the Royal and Ancient Golf Club of Saint Andrews. Then one is advised to seek the middle of the enormous green, taking care to avoid a rather large twenty-foot depression in front known as the Valley of Sin.[1] Allowing players to cross a small burn on their way to the green is the historic Swilcan Bridge. Possibly dating back to the twelfth century, the stone footbridge may have been a gateway to Saint Andrews for pilgrims and packhorses traveling from the old harbor at Guardbridge a few miles away.[2] To cross the bridge is to walk in the footsteps of Old Tom Morris, for whom the hole is named, along with Open champions Jones and Snead, Faldo and Daly, Nicklaus and Woods.

That Winged Foot and Saint Andrews should talk of Revelation and the Valley of Sin could not be more biblical. Whether written as cosmic metaphors to describe creation or from first-hand accounts recounting the life of Christ, the Bible reveals certain truths about God's relationship with us—and ours with God.

For one thing, the Bible is clear that we humans have a tendency to make mistakes. Adam and Eve disobeyed God's instructions in the Garden of Eden. Cain murdered Abel. Things got so bad that God started over again with Noah and the Ark. Moses killed an overseer. David beds Bathsheba. Peter denies Jesus. Judas betrays Christ. Given all this, perhaps the eighteenth at Saint Andrews isn't the only Valley of Sin. The entire planet could qualify. A glance at any newspaper reveals innumerable trespasses from cheating on school tests to lying on tax returns, from adultery to murder, from ignoring the poor to ignoring genocide.

It's not as though we seek to sin. In our weakness, we make poor choices, are tempted easily, fall prey to our bodily desires. Golf is a perfect example. Try as we might, mistakes happen on the course. No golfer addresses the ball on the tee with the express purpose of driving it into the woods, the rough, a quarry, a fairway bunker, a water hazard or out of bounds.

How is it that some of golf's most successful players crash and burn?

Yet, these things happen. Repeatedly.

Jean Van de Velde hits his ball everywhere but on the eighteenth green to fall out of contention in the 1999 British Open at Carnoustie. Greg Norman, after setting a course record 63 at the 1996 Masters, limps home with a 78 in the final round costing him the major. John Daly's career takes a back seat to alcohol.

In the 1968 Masters, Roberto De Vincenzo made what could be called a simple bookkeeping error. On number seventeen at Augusta, the Argentinean tallied a birdie on the par 4 hole. All that was well and good except for the fact that his playing partner, Tommy Aaron, mistakenly entered a four for the hole on the scorecard instead of a three. Partners keep each other's scores then sign their own cards before turning them in to the officials. De Vincenzo did not catch the error. Had he done so, he would have tied Bob Goalby for the 72-hole lead, forcing a playoff for the next day. As it stood, Goalby got the green jacket and De Vincenzo—despite winning the 1967 British Open and the 1970 Bobby Jones Award for sportsmanship—is remembered for his now famous quote, "What a stupid I am."[3]

More recently, Phil Mickelson capped a remarkable run with a remarkable display of another sort. Lefty had won the 2004 Masters, the 2005 PGA and the 2006 Masters. He was also poised to win the 2006 U.S. Open at Winged Foot, which would have given him three majors in a row. Leading by one, with one hole left to play, Mickelson chose to hit a driver on number 18, an odd choice given that he had only hit two of thirteen fairways during the round. Unfortunately, his ball traveled way left, bouncing off the corporate hospitality tent and landing in trampled grass surrounded by trees. Instead of playing a safe second shot, Mickelson took charge only to have his shot hit a tree. His third stroke escaped the mini-forest only to find the greenside bunker. When all was said and shot, he had a double bogey for the hole, handing the lead and the Open to Geoff Ogilvy. Said a frustrated Mickelson, "I still am in shock that I did that. I just can't believe I did that. I am such an idiot."[4]

How is it that some of golf's most successful players, on the cusp of winning major championships, can crash and burn like that?

Often these pages have turned to Saint Andrews for answers. This time, they turn to Saint Peter.

As one of Christ's handpicked apostles, Peter had the opportunity to walk and talk with Jesus as few have had. He was present at the Lord's transfiguration and the raising of Jairus' daughter from the dead, and heard many of the Jesus' teachings. For his part, Peter recognized Jesus' power and divinity. This fisherman so loved the Lord that he often sought to imitate him. Ah, but while the flesh is willing, the spirit is sometimes weak. In this case, Peter failed to carry a water hazard:

> *Immediately Jesus made the disciples get into the boat and go on ahead to the other side.... When evening came, he was there alone, but by this time the boat, battered by the waves, was far from the land, for the wind was against them. And early in the morning he came walking towards them on the lake. But when the disciples saw him walking on the lake, they were terrified, saying, "It is a ghost!" And they cried out in fear. But immediately Jesus spoke to them and said, "Take heart, it is I; do not be afraid."*
>
> *Peter answered him, "Lord, if it is you, command me to come to you on the water." He said, "Come." So Peter got out of the boat, started walking on the water, and came towards Jesus. But when he noticed the strong wind, he became frightened, and beginning to sink, he cried out, 'Lord, save me!'* (Matthew 14:22, 24-31).

How often have we been afraid? How often have we doubted? For that matter, how often have we thought we knew better? Peter, for one, thought nothing of trying to impose his own will over that of Christ's, mistaking his own for the better path: *From that time on, Jesus began to show his disciples that he must go to Jerusalem and undergo great suffering at the hands of the elders and chief priests and scribes, and be killed, and on the third day be raised. And Peter took him aside and began to rebuke him, saying, "God forbid it, Lord! This must never happen to you." But he turned and said to Peter, "Get behind me, Satan! You are a stumbling block to me; for you are setting your mind not on divine things but on human things"* (Matthew 16: 21-23).

If ever there was a person in the Bible to give us hope, it is Peter. Fisherman, brother, husband, well intentioned, headstrong, loyal, weak, faithful, often missing the mark. Peter is a part of us all, a perfect example of what it is to be imperfect. To be human. He fails time and again. And Jesus loves him all the more.

Peter was one of the first to realize Jesus was the Messiah, yet he is called "Satan" for trying to dissuade Jesus from his destiny on the cross. Peter believed so much in Jesus that he asked the Lord to allow him to walk on water. When Christ did so, Peter's own lack of faith caused him to sink. Jesus proclaimed Peter as the rock upon whom he will build his church, yet Peter denied his Lord three times. Despite all this Jesus forgives Peter, restores him, and believes in him so much he entrusts him with his flock.

Given time, patience and, in some cases, help from above, the veil is lifted, a new day dawns, the Light (of the World) goes on. After nine years, Ben Hogan's swing falls into place.[5] People seek to help others and in so doing help themselves. The game is made easy; life is worth living. Arnold Palmer overcomes the death of a good friend in college to eventually resume golfing to become one of the legends of the game.[6] The apostles become the foundation of Christ's church. They spread the Good News that is Jesus, the Word of God. Simon Peter grows from denying Jesus three times to being the one to whom Christ says: *And I tell you, you are Peter, and on this rock I will build my church* (Matthew 16:18).

We are made in the image and likeness of God. We are created out of God's divine imagination. God sustains us with unending love, not only giving us mulligan after mulligan in our lives but also sending his only son to redeem us from our seeming unending tendency to sin.

Jesus foretold of his passion. Matthew, Mark and Luke each noted this fact in the gospels to their respective audiences, it was that important: *He took the twelve aside again and began to tell them what was to happen to him, saying, "See, we are going up to Jerusalem, and the Son of Man will be handed over to the chief priests and to the scribes, and they will condemn him to death; they will hand him over to the Gentiles; they will mock him, and spit upon him, and flog him and kill him; and after three days he will rise again"* (Mark 10:32-34).

And so he was killed. And so he did rise.

Though painful and agonizing, dying was the easy part. Only when Christ rose from the dead did his disciples sense the wonder of it all, realize the miracle and mystery they had been a part of, believe without a doubt that the Son of God had walked in their midst.

So what does it all mean for us? By listening to Christ's words from the cross we learn everything we need to know to be saved: forgive others, take care of one another, thirst for spiritual union, trust in God. By being blessed by the Lord's resurrection we are given the one thing we need to see us through our darkest days: hope. Hope that despite all our fears and failures, our sins and trespasses, our human imperfections, we are forgiven. Hope that despite dreams unrealized, loves unrequited, plans disappointed, children lost, marriages torn, despite our bodies growing old and failing us, we too, through God's mercy and grace, can overcome sin, can overpower death.

Hope that there is, indeed, hope for us.

What's more, as the Bible provides us hope, remarkably so too does golf. Jack Nicklaus overcomes a mild case of polio as a child[7] to become one of the greatest to ever play the game. Tiger Woods, successful though he was, remakes his swing[8] to take advantage of superior club technology, becoming even more a complete player. In each of these cases, the golfers experienced what can be considered a death and resurrection, a good-bye to a former way of being, a rebirth to a new life.

As the Bible provides us hope, remarkably so too does golf.

Two of the game's notable players came close to literally dying and then experienced new lives. By 1949, Ben Hogan had won more than 50 tournaments, including the 1946 and 1948 PGA Championships and the 1948 U.S. Open. However, his career was rudely interrupted on February 1, 1949 on a bridge veiled in heavy fog near the town of Van Horn in west Texas. There, Hogan and his wife Valerie were on the worse side of an auto accident with a Greyhound bus.[9]

Hogan suffered a double fracture of his pelvis, a fracture to his left ankle, a fractured collarbone and a chipped rib. Recovery was threatened by near fatal blood clots. Doctors thought Hogan might never walk again, much less play golf. Think how many moving body parts go into a golf swing. Now compare that to Hogan's list of injuries. Yet, not only did Hogan walk again, he came back swinging on the golf course. Though plagued by circulatory problems for the rest of his life, Hogan made golf look as easy as 1-2-3. Majors, that is. In 1950, he captured one, the U.S. Open. A year later he added two more, the Masters and U.S. Open. Two years after that, he took home another three: another Masters and U.S. Open, plus the British Open.

Lee Trevino faced similar circumstances. Between 1968 and 1974, the Merry Mex won five major tournaments: the U.S. Open in 1968 and 1971, back-to-back British Opens in 1971 and 1972, and the 1974 PGA Championship. During the 1975 Western Open, the Texas ball-striker was struck—by lightning.[10] The subsequent injuries to his back and spine necessitated surgery to remove a damaged disk. Needless to say, his back and his game were never the same. Still, at the age of 44, Trevino added one last major, the 1984 PGA Championship, to his sterling resume.

Just as both Hogan and Trevino enjoyed a rebirth of their game and their fame, so too was Peter given a second chance by the one whom he betrayed: *Now Peter was sitting outside in the courtyard. A servant-girl came to him and said, "You also were with Jesus the Galilean." But he denied it before all of them, saying, "I do not know what you are talking about." When he went out to the porch, another servant-girl saw him, and she said to the bystanders, "This man was with Jesus of Nazareth." Again he denied it with an oath, "I do not know the man." After a little while the bystanders came up and said to Peter, "Certainly you are also one of them, for your accent betrays you." Then he began to curse, and he swore an oath, "I do not know the man!" At that moment the cock crowed. Then Peter remembered what Jesus had said: "Before the cock crows, you will deny me three times." And he went out and wept bitterly* (Matthew 26:69-75).

In a sense it could be said that Peter really didn't know the man. Jesus was someone who government authorities viewed as a rebel, religious leaders saw as sacrilegious and a threat to their power, neighbors mocked, and whose teachings even his intimates could not immediately understand. A man who could heal the sick, give sight to the blind, drive demons out, walk on water, and raise a friend from the dead. A man who predicted his own death and resurrection three days later! Not your average Joseph to say the least. Only when Christ had visited the apostles after his death were all things made clear.

Peter denied his Lord three times, an episode that parallels our own tendency to fail repeatedly despite our best intentions. Though a low point in Peter's life, the event provided Jesus an opportunity to demonstrate God's forgiveness of each of our debts, of every trespass, of all of our sins: *When they had finished breakfast, Jesus said to Simon Peter, "Simon son of John, do you love me more than these?" He said to him, "Yes, Lord; you know that I love you." Jesus said to him, "Feed my lambs." A second time he said to him, "Simon son of John, do you love me?" He said to him, "Yes, Lord; you know that I love you." Jesus said to him, "Tend my sheep." He said to him the third time, "Simon son of John, do you love me?" Peter felt hurt because he said to him the third time, "Do you love me?"*

*And he said to him, "Lord, you know everything; you know that I love you."*
*Jesus said to him, "Feed my sheep"* (John 21:15-17)

Three times did Peter deny Jesus; three times did Christ welcome him home. So too will he welcome us home if only we but knock at his door and say, "My fault."

Even the game of golf exemplifies death and resurrection, forgiveness and rebirth. For every shank, skull, slice and hook, for every ball that lands in the rough or river, trees or traps, bunkers or out of bounds, there is a chance at redemption with the following shot, a prospect of rebirth at the next hole, a possibility of resurrection the next time one takes to the course. Every hole ever played always ends with a good shot, a putt that finds the bottom of the cup from mere inches to hundreds of yards away. A wonderful drive on the third hole. A remarkable chip shot on eight. A winding putt on the fifteenth. A birdie to close the round. There is always one shot somewhere that gives a player hope that their game is improving.

Resurrection gives us a chance at new life. Every day we die to God. It may be by ignoring a homeless person on the street, a cross word to a loved one, an eruption of road rage, a fist thrown in anger, a marriage betrayed. Every day, we also have a chance to be born anew, to rise again, to live as Jesus taught us, to grow closer to God.

To be forgiven. To do good works.

Despite our foils and foibles, our stumbles and tumbles, our sins and trespasses, we are given another chance by the grace of God. On those days we avoid temptation, at those times we overcome our selfishness and give of ourselves to another, there is a feeling of warmth in our hearts. This inner joy is nothing less than the fanning of the life spark of God that lies within each of us.

Golf is not just one hole or one game, just as our life is not just what happens today or this year. Neither is one stop along the way; both are an entire journey. All of us will be faced with trials of one sort or another. Sometimes we avoid life's traps and hazards, sometimes we stumble and fall. All that God asks of us is that we do the best we can each and every time. Either way, it is enough. With success comes rejoicing. With setback comes learning, and the experience to prevail the next time.

Hope.

Sport and spirit provide a never-ending supply of this most valuable virtue. In a world plagued by threats of war, greed, death and disease, the Bible shows us how we should conduct our lives, and where comfort may be found. With every new round, golf affords us all a clean scorecard and renewed confidence with which to set forth for greener pastures. If we falter, should we flail, we are given another chance next shot, next hole, next game. Should we sin against the Father, he too grants us as many "strokes" as we might need to reach the ultimate green that is his kingdom. When we sin, we die to God; when we're forgiven, when we do good works, we are given new life. Forever and ever.

As Jesus said: *"I am the resurrection and the life. Those who believe in me, even though they die, will live, and everyone who lives and believes in me will never die"* (John 11:25-26).

Now that is truly Good News.

# The Clubhouse

After a round of eighteen exhilarating or, depending upon one's skill level, excruciating holes of golf, players retreat to the nineteenth hole—otherwise known as the clubhouse—for congratulations or, depending upon one's skill level, commiseration.

Clubhouses come in all shapes and sizes. Outside the Royal and Ancient Golf Club at Saint Andrews is the most recognizable timepiece in all of golf, the R&A clock tower. Inside is the original Claret Jug, emblematic of the Open Championship. The clubhouse at Oak Hill was first a converted barn lit by kerosene lamps;[1] today it is a grand Tudor edifice. Winged Foot offers a stately stone manor for its clubhouse, while the one at the Dragon at Gold Mountain in the Sierras follows a Frank Lloyd Wright design honoring Native Americans with roofs shaped like teepees.

Structure aside, what makes the nineteenth hole one of the most popular stops on the course is that it provides time and space for reflection about the just-played game, a sharing of experiences at different holes, a comparing of shots and approaches taken by playing partners. Here players realize that golf is more than just the mechanics of a swing or the playing of a course. There is a social component as well. People maintain friendships over eighteen holes weekly. Relationships are formed with strangers when a threesome needs a fourth. In the clubhouse, talk will eventually leave the white ball behind and venture into areas of profession, health, family, dreams, accomplishments and more. Yes, thoughts are exchanged about how to correct a slice. But growth of another kind comes when players discuss how to better relate to a teenaged son who is growing more independent. Or how to deal with parents who can no longer take care of themselves. People are brought closer together by the shared experiences of the up and down on the eighth or the eighteenth hole, as well as the common events that comprise the ups and downs of life. There is even a little something sacramental about the gathering. Bread is broken in the form of cheeseburgers. Wine may be shared.

In this way, the clubhouse resembles a church hall after services. Instead of Arnold Palmer, the man and the beverage, at church you may find the pastor with coffee and donuts. It's a place where people can reflect about the service just attended, the homily just heard. Seeds are planted for the formation of faith-sharing groups or Bible study sessions.

The clubhouse resembles a church hall after services.

Slowly, people realize that there's more to the Christian life than obeying the commandments and attending church regularly. A whole new world opens up with the exposure to community. Invitations are extended to join a men's group, a marriage enrichment ministry or a homelessness committee. Others tell of working with youth or working one night a week at a men's shelter. A cancer victim may disclose how a dark night of the soul gave way to a new appreciation for life.

By meeting and conversing with fellow church members, the

congregation becomes less a structure and more of a community of people. Religion becomes less about rules and more about shared experiences. Spirituality becomes less a singular journey than one taken with others.

For years I kept to myself at church, forgoing any interaction with people before or after. Then one day I was invited to serve on a parish time and talent committee. To use biblical language, that begat involvement in the faith formation committee which begat participation with a parish newcomers team which begat being a Eucharistic minister which begat leading a social justice exploration which begat tutoring children of immigrants.

By becoming involved, taking small steps on a spiritual journey, I have had a change of heart. Before I viewed the church as an institution that told me what not to do. Now I view the church as a community that shows what is possible to do. It's as if all my hooks and slices have now been made straight off the tee. Instead of being a loner on the driving range, I am a member of a vibrant club.

I hope by the "playing" of these eighteen holes you have had an enjoyable round of golf, as well as a welcoming introduction to the Bible. Just as we need to learn how to read the greens to putt successfully, so too do we need to read the Good Book to understand the contours of our lives. A common theme runs through the game and the Bible. In golf, the more we practice and hone our drives, chips and putts, the more successful we become on the fairways and greens. With regard to our soul, the more we practice our faith, discern our purpose, do good works, live lives of kindness and service, the closer we come to God. So, nurture your talents, avoid the valley of sin, and reserve your heavenly tee time today.

# Another Round?

As a young, sports-loving, Catholic boy growing up near San Francisco, my early life was made up of equal parts evening prayers and morning scores, holy cards and baseball cards, biographies of saints and sluggers. As gospel evangelists Matthew and Mark took hold of my soul, San Francisco Giants Mays and McCovey captured my heart. There was even a touch of the here and hereafter associated with the sponsor of one of my Little League teams: Chapel of the Highlands Mortuary.

Over the years my love of sports and curiosity about Scripture deepened. So much so that they (miraculously perhaps) came together in a book entitled, *And God Said, "Play Ball!" — Amusing and Thought-Provoking Parallels Between the Bible and Baseball.* Themes of forgiveness, reconciliation, service, inclusion, prayer and more were explored through stories of biblical Ruth and Babe Ruth, Joseph of Egypt and Joseph of DiMaggio, Moses and Aaron (Hank, that is), Yogi Berra, Jesus Christ and others. *Catholic New York* called it "intelligent and illuminating," the national Catholic newspaper *Our Sunday Visitor* found it a "delightful read," and my mom thought it was "really good."

Thankfully, the project was a success. In fact my editor, Paul Pennick, suggested a follow up. Thus, *And God Said, "It's Good!"* was born, exploring the parallels between faith and football. It's Good lived up to its name with tales of Hail Mary prayers and passes, Immaculate Conceptions and receptions, biblical verses and double reverses, redemptions of careers and lives, tales of the Saints (both those wearing halos and those donning helmets), and more.

There are good reasons why thousands of people have been

drawn to these books. Not the least of which is that, like people, God could very easily be a sports fan. Think about the opening words to the Bible: *In the beginning.* For all we know, the author may have misunderstood the Almighty's divine instructions. What may have really been said was, "In the big inning." Hard to believe? Then consider that after creating the world in six days, God rested on the seventh. Why? It very well could have been that Our Creator rested on Sunday so eons later he could kick back and watch sports.

Kidding aside, what I believe attracts readers to these books, and what inspires me to write them, is seeing God in the everyday. What better place to find joy and the one who is joy to the world than in the games we play. It is my hope that these games can become a lens through which we learn about the word of God. And that by studying the Bible and baseball, or faith and football, or spirituality and golf, we come to a greater appreciation of both sport and Spirit.

I don't know what sport my next book will be about. It could be soccer or basketball, hockey or tennis. Who knows, with my son now playing lacrosse that topic could be ripe for exploration. What I do know is that I look forward to being moved again by the Spirit to uncover further connections among games we love and the God who loves us.

Gary Graf
Seattle, Washington

# Sources and Permissions

Scripture references are taken from the *New Revised Standard Version Bible: Catholic Edition*, copyright 1993 by the Division of Christian Education of the National Council of Churches of Christ in the U.S.A. Used by permission. All rights reserved.

Sources for information on the golf holes described in this book come from primarily three sources: *The 500 World's Greatest Golf Holes* by George Peper and the Editors of GOLF Magazine (Artisan, 2003); www.golfclubatlas.com; and the Web sites of the individual golf courses mentioned.

All golfing statistics come primarily from the Web sites of the four major golf tournaments: Masters, U.S. Open, British Open and PGA Championship. All efforts have been made to reflect these statistics accurately. Please accept my apologies for any errors that may have inadvertently occurred.

NOTES

FIRST HOLE

1. www.hotel-online.com/News/PR2005_4th/ Nov05_KPMGGolfSurvey.html
2. en.wikipedia.org/wiki/golf
3. Ibid.
4. www.unep.org/geo2000/english/0045.htm
5. www.factmonster.com/ipka/A0934288.html
6. www.nefsc.noaa.gov/faq
7. www.factmonster.com/ipka/A0934288.html
8. www.cnn.com/2003/TECH/space/07/22/stars.survey
9. www.prestwickgc.co.uk/history.html
10. Ibid.

11. www.prestwickgc.co.uk/course.html
12. www.chcc.com/Default.aspx?=DynamicModule&pageid=223314&ssid=69989&vnf=1

SECOND HOLE

1. www.prairiedunes.com
2. www.prairiedunes.com/club_history.shtml
3. www.thinkbabynames.com/meaning/0/Khadija
4. www.babynamecountry.com/meanings/Kadijah.html
5. www.pinehurst.com/new/pdfs/PHNo2-timeline.pdf
6. Ibid.

THIRD HOLE

1. www.gohawaii.com/big-island
2. www.tcclub.org/Club/Scripts/public/public.asp
3. en.wikipedia.org/wiki/The_Country_Club
4. www.worldgof.com/golf-history/us-open-golf-champions-through-history-2295.htm
5. www.golfclubatlas.com/thecountryclub1.html
6. www.oakmont-countryclub.org/Default.aspx?p=DynamicModule&pageid=233849&ssid=86046&vnf=1
7. www.golf.about.com/od/golfcoursearchitecture/f/church_pews.htm
8. Peper, George, and the Editors of Golf Magazine, *The 500 World's Greatest Golf Holes*, (Artisan, 2003), page 160.
9. Eyewitness Travel Guides, Paris, (Dorling Kindersley, London, 1993), page 89.
10. en.wikipedia.org/wiki/Arnold_Palmer_(drink)

FOURTH HOLE

1. usga.usopen.com/history/index.html
2. www.pga.com/pgaofamerica/history/1910-1919.html

3. www.pgatour.com/tournaments/r033/index.html

4. www.masters.org/en_US/history/index.html

5. en.wikipedia.org/wiki/Grand_Slam_of_golf

## FIFTH HOLE

1. www.pgatour.com/tournaments/r021/course.html

2. www.since1895.com/since1895.html

3. en.wikipedia.org/wiki/Payne_Stewart

4. www.masters.org/en_US/history/results/1996.html

5. en.wikipedia.org/wiki/Greg_Norman

## SIXTH HOLE

1. www.wfgc.info/html/frameset.html

2. Merriam Webster Dictionary, Apple MacBook dashboard.

3. Peper, page 260.

4. en.wikipedia.org/wiki/Carnoustie_Golf_Links

5. Ibid.

6. www.opengolf.com/history/past_opens.sps?PartNo=136

7. www.opengolf.com/history/past_opens.sps?PartNo=128

8. news.bbc.co.uk/1/hi/sport/golf/397813.stm

9. en.wikipedia.org/wiki/Carnoustie_Golf_Links

10. www.pgatour.com/players/00/22/13 and en.wikipedia.org/wiki/
    Lee_Trevino

## SEVENTH HOLE

1. www.golfclubatlas.com/sandhills.html

2. findarticles.com/p/articles/mi_m4070/is_2001_May/ai_74829987 ("You
   can go home again—Pebble Beach Golf Links" by John Steinbreder)

3. Killgallon, Rev. James, and Weber, Rev. Gerard, *Life in Christ*, ACTA
   Publications, 1995, pages 244-246.

EIGHTH HOLE

1. Peper, page 289.

2. www.royaltroon.co.uk/courses/postagestamp.htm

3. www.opengolf.com/history/claret_jug.sps

4. en.wikipedia.org/wiki/claret

NINTH HOLE

1. www.pebblebeach.com/page.asp?/id=1332

TENTH HOLE

1 www.therivieracountryclub.com/html/history.cfm?history_ID=2

2. www.therivieracountryclub.com/html/history.cfm?history_ID=1

3. www.golfclubatlas.com/pinevalley1.html

4. Ibid.

5. en.wikipedia.org/wiki/Pine_Valley_Golf_Club

6. www.golfdom.com/golfdom/article/articleDetail.jsp?id=337606 ("Wise Beyond His Years" by Thomas Skemivitz)

7. Ibid.

8. www.golfclubatlas.com/wingedfoot000188.html

9. www.golfclubatlas.com/pinevalley1.html; Peper, page 301.

ELEVENTH HOLE

1. www.usopen.com/2006/history/pastchamps/1932.html

2. Peper, page 435.

3. en.wikipedia.org/wiki/Old_Course_at_St_Andrews

4. Ibid.

5. www.standrew.org.uk/golf/the_courses_/old_guide2004/ old_course_hole_guide_11.html

6. Peper, page 118.

7. www.catholic.org/saints/saints_phpsaint_id=1011

8. www.en.wikipedia.org/wiki/St._George

9. www.saints.sqpn.com/saintg12.htm

10. www.experiencefestival.com/saint-nom-la-bretche_-_history

11. Peper, page 261.

12. www.catholic.org/saints/saint_php?saint_id=50

13. www.catholic.org/saints/saint_php?saint_id=100

TWELFTH HOLE

1. www.en.wikipedia.org/wiki/Chicago_Golf_Club

2. www.golfclubatlas.com/chicago000157.html

3. Peper, page 58.

4. www.masters.org/en_US/history/index.html

5. www.masters.org/en_US/course/index.html

6. www.masters.org/en_US/course/index.html

7  www.masters.org/en_US/history/records/highest.html#hl_hole12

8. Ibid.

THIRTEENTH HOLE

1. www.masters.org/en_US/course/landmarks.html#Amen

2. www.augusta.com/masters2004/stories/040704/his_655332.shtml
("Arnie Says Amen for ruling at 12" by John Boyette, *The Augusta Chronicle*)

FOURTEENTH HOLE

1. www.nicklaus.com/design/facts.php

2. www.golfclubatlas.com/shinnecock1.html

3. www.standrews.org.uk/golf/the_courses/old_course_hole_names.html

4. www.nottsgolfunion.com/interview_jn.htm

5. en.wikipedia.org/wiki/Ben_Hogan

6. www.golf.about.com/cs/beginnersguide/a/which14clubs.htm

7. en.wikipedia.org/wiki/John_Daly_(golfer)

8. www.golf.about.com/od/golfersmen/p/john_daly.htm

FIFTEENTH HOLE

1. Peper, page 10.
2. Eyewitness Travel Guides, Rome, (Dorling Kindersley, London, 1996), pp. 244-245.

SIXTEENTH HOLE

1. www.essortment.com/all/meriongolfclub_rlxs.htm
2. en.wikipedia.org/wiki/Grand_Slam_(golf)
3. Peper, page 32.
4. www.memberstatements.com/tour/tours.cfm?tourid=40648
5. Peper, page 158.
6. www.masters.org/en_US/history/results/1987.html
7. www.sports.espn.go.com/golf/masters08/columns/ story?columnist=harig_bob&id=3326522
8. www.youtube.com/watch?v=qoT_xsrRoIs
9. www.pebblebeach.com/page.asp?id=1427
10. Ibid.
11. www.sports.jrank.org/pages/5156/Watson-Tom-Nicklaus-Shot.html
12. www.masters.org/en_US/history/results/1935.html

SEVENTEENTH HOLE

1. www.carnoustiegolflinks.co.uk/?page_id=209
2. www.scotlands-golf-courses.com/courses/details.asp?cid=101
3. Peper, page 52.
4. en.wikipedia.org/wiki/Bobby_Jones_(golf)
5. en.wikipedia.org/wiki/Walter_Hagen
6. en.wikipedia.org/wiki/Gene_Sarazen
7. en.wikipedia.org/wiki/Byron_Nelson
8. en.wikipedia.org/wiki/Ben_Hogan
9. Ibid.

10. en.wikipedia.org/wiki/Byron_Nelson

11. en.wikipedia.org/wiki/Tiger_Woods

12. uk.eurosport.yahoo.com/070811/2/umhf.html

13. www.youtube.com/watch?v=1nJfhUGM4Yc

14. en.wikipedia.org/wiki/Payne_Stewart_Award

15. www.garyplayer.com/foundation

16. www.southerncompany.com/aboutus/paynestewartward.asp

17. en.wikipedia.org/wiki/Tiger_Woods

18. www.pgatour.com/players/00/12/49

EIGHTEENTH HOLE

1. www.standrews.org.uk/golf/the_courses/old_guide2004/old_course_hole_guide_18.html

2. www.standrews.org.uk/welcome/faq/index.html

3. en.wikipedia.org/wiki/Roberto_DeVicenzo

4. www.sports.espn.go.com/golf/usopen06/news/story?id=2490383
("Ogilvy wins U.S. Open as Mickelson falters on 18," Associated Press)

5. en.wikipedia.org/wiki/Ben_Hogan

6. en.wikipedia.org/wiki/Arnold_Palmer

7. en.wikipedia.org/wiki/Jack_Nicklaus

8. en.wikipedia.org/wiki/Tiger_Woods

9. en.wikipedia.org/wiki/Ben_Hogan

10. en.wikipedia.org/wiki/Lee_Trevino

NINETEENTH HOLE

1. www.oakhillcc.com/default.aspx?p=DynamicModule&pageid=262791&ssid=127300&vnf=1

# Indices

INDEX OF GOLF COURSES MENTIONED

Augusta National Golf Club, Augusta, Georgia 12, 14, 15, 35, 42, 49, 55, 71, 90, 110-111, 120-121, 125, 133, 149, 157, 165, 171, 177-178

Baltimore Country Club, Lutherville, Maryland 90

Baltusrol Golf Club, Springfield, New Jersey 13, 15, 20, 42, 57, 88, 99

Banff Springs Golf Course, Banff, Alberta, Canada 15

Bay Hill Club, Orlando, Florida 15, 125

Bel-Air Country Club, Los Angeles, California 87

Bethpage State Park Golf Club, Farmingdale, New York 15, 32, 39-40, 41, 53, 88

Brook Hollow Golf Club, Dallas, Texas 88

Bruntsfield Links, Edinburgh, Scotland 10

Carnoustie Golf Links, Carnoustie, Angus, Scotland 32, 58, 59, 72, 159-160, 162, 177

Cherry Hills Country Club, Cherry Hills Village, Colorado 7, 17-18, 35

Chicago Golf Club, Wheaton, Illinois 109

Colonial Country Club, Fort Worth, Texas 49

The Country Club, Chestnut Hill, Massachusetts 29-30

Crystal Downs County Club, Frankfort, Michigan 71

Cypress Point Club, Pebble Beach, California 12, 14, 15, 71, 111, 134, 145

Desert Mountain Golf Club, Scottsdale, Arizona 133

Doral Resort and Country Club, Miami, Florida 15

Dragon at Gold Mountain, Clio, California 187

Firestone Country Club, Akron, Ohio 15

Gary Player Country Club, Sun City, South Africa 125

Grand Cypress Resort, Orlando, Florida 67

The Greenbier, White Sulphur Springs, West Virginia 14

Hapuna Golf Course, Big Island, Hawaii 32

Harbour Town Golf Links, Hilton Head Island, South Carolina 32, 125

Hazeltine National Golf Club, Chaska, Minnesota 42, 50

The Inverness Club, Toledo, Ohio 15, 150

Kemper Lakes Golf Club, Kildeer, Illinois 50

Links at Spanish Bay, Pebble Beach, California 125

Loch Lomond Golf Club, Luss, Dumbartonshire, Scotland 125

Long Cove Club, Hilton Head Island, South Carolina 32

The Maidstone Club, East Hampton, New York 79

Mauna Kea Golf Club, Big Island, Hawaii 12, 15, 29, 32

Medinah Country Club, Medinah, Illinois 23, 24, 42

Merion Golf Club, Ardmore, Pennsylvania 59, 128, 145
Muirfield, Gullane, East Lothian, Scotland 35, 72
Muirfield Village Golf Club, Dublin, Ohio 15, 35, 125-127
The National Golf Links of America, Southhampton, New York 12, 40,
    57, 79
Newport Country Club, Newport, Rhode Island 41
North Berwick Golf Club, North Berwick, East Lothian, Scotland 40
Oak Hill Country Club, Rochester, New York 35, 42, 63, 65, 67, 119, 187
Oak Tree Golf Club, Edmond, Oklahoma 12
Oakland Hills Country Club, Bloomfield Hills, Michigan 35, 146-148
Oakmont Country Club, Oakmont, Pennsylvania 15, 30-32, 34, 35, 41, 59
Olympic Club, San Francisco, California 67
Pebble Beach Golf Links, Pebble Beach, California 32, 41, 66-67, 71-72,
    150, 157, 170, 175
Pine Valley Golf Club, Clementon, New Jersey 59, 88, 90, 119, 133
Pinehurst Country Club, Pinehurst, North Carolina 15, 20, 24, 27, 32, 41,
    49, 50
The Pines at The International, Bolton, Massachusetts 13
Prairie Dunes Country Club, Hutchinson, Kansas 23, 27
Prestwick Golf Club, Prestwick, Ayrshire, Scotland 9, 15, 16, 18, 41
The Riviera County Club, Pacific Palisades, California 87
Royal Melbourne Golf Club, Black Rock, Victoria, Australia 14, 71
Royal St. George's Golf Club, Sandwich, Kent, England 105
Royal Troon Golf Club, Troon, Ayrshire, Scotland 72, 72, 167
St. Andrews (Old), St. Andrews, Fife, Scotland 7, 13, 15, 16, 32-33, 48, 72,
    90, 100-101-102, 104, 127, 131, 133, 162, 176-177, 179, 187
St. Enodoc, Wadebridge, Cornwall, England 105
St. George's Golf and Country Club, Etobicoke, Ontario, Canada 105
St. Germaine Golf Club, Saint-Germain-En-Laye, France 105
St. Louis Country Club, St. Louis, Missouri 104-105
St. Nom La Bretèche Golf Club, St. Nom La Bretèche, France 105
San Francisco Golf Club, San Francisco, California 67, 88, 106
Sand Hills Club, Mullen, Nebraska 15, 65, 67, 72, 134
Saucon Valley Country Club, Bethlehem, Pennsylvania 59
Shinnecock Hills Golf Club, Southhampton, New York 41, 57, 79, 99-100,
    126-127
Siwanoy Country Club, Bronxville, New York 42
Somerset Hills Country Club, Bernardsville, New Jersey 88-89
Southern Hills Country Club, Tulsa, Oklahoma 7, 41, 42, 109-110

Spyglass Hill Golf Club, Pebble Beach, California 7, 15, 17-18, 32, 39, 80, 81

Torrey Pines Golf Club, La Jolla, California 41

Tournament Player's Club at Sawgrass, Ponte Vedra Beach, Florida 15, 33, 159-160

Turnberry Golf Club, Turnberry, Ayrshire, Scotland 35

Winged Foot Golf Club, Mamaroneck, New York 13, 15, 20, 41, 42, 57, 88-89, 95, 175-176, 178, 187

Yale Golf Course, New Haven, Connecticut 79, 81, 83

## INDEX OF HOLES AND HAZARDS MENTIONED

Allen's Creek 119

Alps 12

Amen Corner 7, 10, 120-121

Azalea 111, 120

Beast 59

Billie Burn 159

Blind Pew 39

Camellia 111

Captain Smollett 80

Cherry 111

Church Pews 9, 31-32, 34

Devil's A_hole 88

Duel 106

Eden Estuary 14, 101

Genesis 13

Glacier Bunker 39

Golden Bell 112

Greist Pond 79

Hell Bunker 127

Hell's Half Acre 9-10, 88, 90

Hill Bunker 101, 127

Himalayas 13

Horrible Horseshoe 49

Island Green 6

Island Hole 159

Jockie's Burn 59

Juniper 111

Kadijah 23

Long 59

Magnolia 111

Monster 147

Pink Dogwood 111

Postage Stamp 6, 73

Pulpit 9, 88-89

Punch Bowl 6, 109

Quarry 146

Rae's Creek 112, 120

Railway 16

Redbud 111, 171

Road Bunker 160

Road Hole 160

Sahara 59, 90

Saharas 13

Strath Bunker 101

Swilcan Bridge 176

Trinity River 49

Trouble 57

Valley of Sin 7, 9, 176-177

White Dogwood 111

White Faces 145

Yale Bowl 79

Yellow Jasmine 111

## INDEX OF GOLFERS AND
## COURSE DESIGNERS MENTIONED

**Aaron, Tommy** 178
**Anderson, Willie** 99
**Ballesteros, Seve** 100, 111
**Bolt, Tommy** 7, 109
**Boros, Julius** 30, 89
**Braid, James** 73, 164
**Cabrera, Angel** 31
**Campbell, Michael** 50
**Casper, Billy** 57
**Colt, Harry** 88
**Coore, Bill** 65
**Crenshaw, Ben** 15, 65, 111
**Crump, George** 88
**Daly, John** 7-8, 13, 34, 101, 131-132, 173, 176, 177
**Davis, William** 126
**De Vincenzo, Roberto** 177-178
**DeMaret, Jimmy** 111
**Dye, Peter** 159
**Egan, H. Chandler** 175
**Elkington, Steve** 87
**Els, Ernie** 31
**Faldo, Nick** 56, 74, 100, 111, 176
**Floyd, Raymond** 100, 109
**Flynn, William** 126
**Foulis, James** 100
**Fownes, Henry and William** 31, 88
**Garcia, Sergio** 58
**Gibson, Kelley** 173
**Goalby, Bob** 178
**Goosen, Retief** 100, 109
**Graham, David** 147
**Grant, Douglas** 175
**Green, Hubert** 109
**Hagen, Walter** 33, 66, 72, 74, 78, 147, 165-166, 172
**Harrington, Padraig** 58
**Hogan, Ben** 24, 30, 32, 33, 42-43, 49, 87, 110, 111, 128, 131, 146, 147, 166-168, 172-73, 180, 182-183
**Irwin, Hale** 23, 57

Janzen, Lee 99
Jones, Bobby 30, 33, 41, 57, 100, 110, 111, 125, 145-146, 150, 165, 172, 176
Jones, Sr., Robert Trent 15, 29, 39, 67
Jones, Steve 147
Langer, Bernhard 111
Lawrie, Paul 58
Leonard, Justin 58, 72
Littler, Gene 147
Locke, Bobby 74
Love, III, Davis 49, 57
Lyle, Sandy 150
MacDonald, Charles Blair 88
MacKenzie, Alister 14, 71, 87, 88, 111, 134, 165
Manero, Tony 99
Maxwell, Perry 23
Mediate, Rocco 41
Mickelson, Phil 33, 99, 102, 111, 121, 178
Middlehoff, Dr. Cary 66
Miller, Johnny 30, 33, 35
Mize, Larry 149-150, 156
Morris, Tom (the elder) 16, 176
Morris, Tom (the younger) 16, 72
Nelson, Byron 10, 33, 111, 149, 166-168, 172-173
Neville, Jack 175
Nicklaus, Jack 15, 24, 30, 32, 33, 35-36, 43, 59, 66, 67, 74, 99, 100, 111, 125, 127, 131, 133, 146, 147, 149, 150, 167, 168-173, 176, 182
Norman, Greg 55-56, 149-150, 177
North, Andy 147
Ogilvie, Geoff 57, 178
Olazabal, Jose Maria 111
Ouimet, Francis 30
Palmer, Arnold 15, 17, 32, 33, 35, 42, 72, 111, 114, 120-121, 125, 147, 168-169, 172-173, 180, 188
Pavin, Corey 100
Player, Gary 32, 33, 35, 43, 59, 111, 114, 125, 147, 148, 166, 168-169, 172-173
Price, Nick 109, 131
Ray, Ted 30
Roberts, Clifford 110
Rocca, Costantino 131
Ross, Donald 15, 24, 49, 66, 88, 146

**Sarazen, Gene** 30, 33, 42-43, 101, 151, 157, 165-166, 172

**Shute, Denny** 50, 101

**Smith, Horton** 43, 111

**Snead, Sam** 24, 30, 32, 33, 100, 111, 149, 166-168, 172, 176

**Stewart, Payne** 50, 173

**Stockton, Dave** 7, 109

**Storm, Graeme** 7

**Strange, Curtis** 30, 66, 112

**Sutton, Hal** 87, 173

**Taylor, John Henry** 164

**Thomas, George C.** 87-88

**Thomson, Peter** 74

**Tillinghast, Albert (A.W.)** 14-15, 39, 57, 67, 88, 99, 106

**Toms, David** 173

**Toomey, Howard** 126

**Trevino, Lee** 33, 35-36, 62-53, 66, 114, 146, 150, 169-170, 172, 183

**Tway, Bob** 150

**Van de Velde, Jean** 57-58, 177

**Vardon, Harry** 20, 72, 78, 164-165, 172

**Wadkins, Lanny** 49

**Watson, Tom** 32, 33, 35-36, 72, 73, 78, 111, 125, 150-151, 157, 160, 162, 169-170, 172

**Weiskopf, Tom** 72, 112, 125

**Wilson, Hugh** 145

**Woods, Tiger** 7-8, 13, 16, 23, 32, 35, 39, 41, 42-43, 74, 101-101, 111, 131, 147, 149, 167, 170-173, 176, 182

**Zaharias, Babe Didrikson** 24

**Zarley, Kermit** 150

**Zoeller, Fuzzy** 57

# Also for Sports Fans

### AND GOD SAID, "PLAY BALL!"
**Amusing and Thought-Provoking Parallels
between the Bible and Baseball**
by Gary Graf

The best-selling book on the connections between baseball and the Bible, by the author of *And God Said, "Tee it up!"* (180-page paperback, $14.95)

### AND GOD SAID, "IT'S GOOD!"
**Amusing and Thought-Provoking Parallels
between the Bible and Football**
by Gary Graf

The best-selling book on the connections between football and the Bible, by the author of *And God Said, "Tee it up!"* (181-page hardcover, $19.95)

### THE BOOK OF SPORTS VIRTUES
**Portraits from the Field of Play**
by Fritz Knapp, with illustrations by Tommy Edwards

Portraits of famous athletes who exhibited the virtues of appreciation, compassion, dedication, honesty strength, humility, integrity, nobility, persistence, discipline, triumph, trust, unity, wisdom and determination. (239-page leatherette cover, $14.95)

### DIAMOND PRESENCE
**12 Stories of Finding God at the Old Ball Park**
edited by Gregory F. Augustine Pierce

Twelve true stories by accomplished writers who discovered the presence of God at a ballpark as a player, coach, parent, child or just plain fan. (175-page hardcover, $17.95)

### THE BALLGAME OF LIFE
**Lessons for Parents and Coaches of Young Baseball Players**
by David Allen Smith and Joseph Aversa, Jr.

A book for parents and coaches who love baseball and want to be involved in encouraging children to learn and enjoy it. (125-page paperback, $9.95)

**Available from booksellers or 800-397-2282
www.actapublications.com**